THE
SEVEN
PILLARS
of PARENTING

THE
SEVEN
PILLARS
of PARENTING

Raising a Champion Child
in a World without Boundaries

LINDA OREM HORTON

Oviedo, Florida

The Seven Pillars of Parenting
by Linda Orem Horton

Published by HigherLife Development Services, Inc.
2342 Westminster Terrace
Oviedo, Florida 32765
(407) 563-4806
www.ahigherlife.com

Unless otherwise identified, Scripture quotations are from the King James Version (KJV) of the Bible.

Scripture quotations marked AMP are taken from the Amplified Bible, Copyright © 1954, 1958, 1962, 1964, 1965, 1987 by The Lockman Foundation. (www. Lockman.org).

ISBN 13: 978-1-935245-01-8
ISBN 10: 1-935245-01-5

Cover Design: Judith McKittrick Wright

First Edition

09 10 11 12 13 — 5 4 3 2 1

Printed in the United States of America

Dedication

*This book is lovingly dedicated to my spiritual mothers:
Mama Lee, Mama Opal, Pastor Claudette, and my dear
Grandma, Lorene Knight Orem. Each one of you is a true
Titus two woman! This book is a tribute to your unending
patience, unconditional love, and immovable faith in God.
You saved my life and I love you all more than words can say.*

Appreciation

I WANT TO EXPRESS LASTING and affectionate appreciation to my beloved husband, Dennis, who is the most loving and thoughtful gift that God could ever give me. You have taught me more about life and about God than you could ever know! I am forever grateful.

To my loving sons, Mathew, Mark, Michael and Timothy—my mighty men of God! No mother has been more blessed. Because of you I strived to do better and because of your love and compassion, I knew I would make it. I love you all so much! You are my heartbeat.

To my beautiful daughters-in-love, Amber and Tiffany—my daughters and my friends. You started as a prayer and ended as my friends. God is faithful! When he gave you to us, he gave us love, laughter, and fun! Each of you has enhanced our family and blessed my life. I love you!

Table of Contents

Wisdom hath builded her house, she hath hewn out her seven pillars.

Proverbs 9:1

Introduction

THIS BOOK IS WRITTEN for anyone who wants to enhance their marriage and improve their relationship with their children of all ages. I firmly believe that if we apply the wonderful common-sense principals written in the Bible, we can build successful family relationships. You will find in these pages the words of a mother and, therefore, my approach with you is straightforward and real. While I am not your birth mother, I will (if you don't mind) in these coming pages be your spiritual mother. If at times I sound hard, don't despair! Sometimes it takes a mom who will love her children enough to keep teaching the reality of truth until that truth becomes a reality. Remember, I love you and I am praying for you. As you read these pages, it is my sincere prayer that you find peace, content-ment, and success in every area of your life. I am a mom; that is what I do.

As I pastored children and their families in the church and school classroom over the years, my heart went out to parents who had no one to talk to and nowhere to turn for help concerning their desperate family situations. Many precious parents were struggling with children who were behaving badly—children who were asserting authority in the home that was not biblically theirs.

We weren't born knowing how to parent—we learn by seeing and by doing. Most of us were raised by well-meaning yet flawed parents. For various reasons and in various ways, most of us have great gaps in our parenting skills. Years ago, I was in the same condition as many parents are today. I came from a churchgoing family, had a typical childhood, and yet my parenting skills were lacking and I was frustrated by how little I knew about being a loving and compassionate mother and wife.

I was in serious trouble and didn't know how to get out of it. True to His Word, God sent me women from all walks of life who took the time to teach me not only about being a mother and a wife, but about how to be a woman of God. They taught me how to be a woman who was more concerned about others than herself; a woman who cared what happened to other families like her own; a woman who wanted to rise above the norm and raise her children differently than she had been raised. My transformation didn't happen overnight—not even in a few years—but it did happen. God is concerned about us and, if we are teachable, He will send someone to teach us what we need to learn.

My life has now come full circle. Now I am honored to follow in the footsteps of the spiritual mothers who saved my life. Thanks to their patient love and teaching, I am now a teacher and a mother to all who are in need of love, care, and guidance. I humbly acknowledge and honor those who taught me by passing on the wisdom and love that was planted in me. Those seeds, planted in love, grew strong in the good soil of obedience and sacrifice. They formed great branches of experience and wisdom. It is on these branches I invite all who need rest to come and lodge.

You will find that I wrote this book honestly—you'll see how I am in real life. You'll see my mistakes and triumphs. I've grown into a mom who loves her children enough to give them truth then keep teaching until the truth becomes reality. I am a mom who has made mistakes and has learned from them—a mom who stands by her kids no matter what. I am a mom who is still learning, even though my children are all adults. And I am a wife who was never taught how to be a good wife. I messed up early and was too stubborn to admit it. I'm a wife who got a second, third, and fourth chance and eagerly took advantage of each chance to make a change for the better. I am a wife who is grateful for the women who have taught me how to be the godly wife I was meant to be.

So, please . . . come. Lodge on the branches and rest. Rest in the knowledge that you are loved and valued. We can all be better wives, husbands, parents, and grandparents. It is never too late to learn and improve. Open these pages sit for a while. Let me love on you and pour into your life the wisdom of a mother, one page at a time, one issue at a time. Together we can do it!

The First Pillar

The Pillar of Priority

And Jesus answered him, "The first of all the commandments is, 'Hear, O Israel; The LORD our God is one LORD: And thou shalt love the LORD thy God with all thy heart, and with all thy soul, and with all thy mind, and with all thy strength': this is the first commandment. And the second is like, namely this, 'Thou shalt love thy neighbour as thyself.' There is none other commandment greater than these."

Mark 12:29-33

In a family, there is a definite godly order:
God is first.
Our spouse is second.
Our children are third.
This order is non-negotiable.

Priority #1: GOD

When we say that God is first in our lives, we must clarify what we mean by God. God is God—alone. We are not talking about our church, our pastor, or our ministry; we are talking about our relationship with our Creator, the Lover of our souls, the One who knew us before our parents knew us, the One who formed us in our mother's womb, the Alpha and Omega, God.

Too many of us confuse church with God. A church is where we worship God; it is not our God. We all get busy and just do...whatever it is...we just do. And in the "do" of life, we forget that God is a "who"—not a place or a what. Spending time together is important in any loving relationship. Our relationship with God is no different. We need to spend time with God, learn His ways, His will, His desires for us and for those around us.

If we look back at when we first got married and get really honest, most of us would say that that first year was a real eye-opener! We are instantly living day and night with someone we really don't know on an intimate level. But we have the opportunity in that relationship to get to know our spouse in a more intimate way than we have ever known anyone in our entire lives.

A couple who have spent a lot of time together and have gotten to know each other intimately on every level will finish each other's sentences or not say a word and know instinctively what the other person is thinking. Words are not needed when a wink can say a multitude!

I was the only girl in my family and had never shared a bed with anyone...ever. I was shocked when I married Dennis at just how much of the bed he took up! Getting accustomed to sharing my space took some time. But over the years, I learned to love having someone else on the other side of the bed, as I listen to the hum of his breathing or feel my husband's hand touch mine in the middle of the night. Yes, he still takes up too much of the bed, but I wouldn't have it any other way.

This is what God had in mind when He created us—a union between Him and us. God started this world in a relationship so that as the years go by, we not only become accustomed to Him, but yearn to become more intimate with Him. We are at peace with who we are with Him and want to learn more about Him each passing day. We will never be alone again because He is our constant companion.

Sadly, too many times, God is not first in our lives. When that happens, we become self-centered, not God-centered. When we are self-centered, we think only of ourselves, making everything we do or say about us and us alone. Friend, I spent too many years in that condition—self-absorbed, self-centered, and just plain selfish. I wasn't the great loving wife, parent, or friend that God had created me to be from the beginning of time. In many eyes, including my own, I was hopeless—but thank God, I started making time for the One who made time!

Please, don't think I sat around all day thinking of myself. Oh, no! I spent plenty of time working in and for the church, working outside our home, and doing community projects. But if I was being totally truthful, I would tell you I wasted so much time thinking about how everything I did made me feel or how it affected me, that I was no good to the ministries or the people I served.

My love, that is what Jesus calls hay and stubble. I had built my spiritual house with hay and stubble, just like one of the three little pigs' houses, and we all know how that turned out for them, don't we!

When we put God first in our lives, we naturally put others first. Love never fails. Maybe that is because God is love and the closer we get to true love, the more we learn to love unconditionally. We no longer care what's in it for us, but sincerely want to facilitate what God wants to do through us for someone else.

Now, this does not mean that we totally take no interest in ourselves. When we don't get enough rest, don't eat right, or get too stressed, we are of no good to anyone, especially God. So many of us are striving to serve the Lord and raise a family, wearing ten different hats all at the same time. We do all of this while stressing and stretching ourselves to the breaking point. Beloved, that is not what God has in mind for His children!

For God so loved the world, that he gave his only begotten Son.

John 3:16

It is only right that we love ourselves enough to stop and take some time to take care of the one that God loved so much. So take the time to have a nutritious lunch and a little rest, and at the end of the day, indulge in an overflowing steaming hot, relaxing bubble bath. If the fancy strikes you (like it often does me), go to the secret hiding place and get some of the good chocolate and don't feel bad! God loves us and wants the best for us. He knows we need to rest, and He doesn't mind our eating the good chocolate once in a while.

What God does not intend is for us to become professional martyrs. One of the definitions of "martyr" is "a great or constant sufferer." We all know someone who fits that definition—always suffering because of the constant forceful striving the person is doing for his or her family, work, or even church. With that person's great sacrifices come great complaining, loud sighs, and downcast, pitiful expressions of woe.

This poor soul we just described is not putting God first (or anyone else, for that matter). This person is really putting himself or herself first. Please trust me when I say this: I came from a long line of sighers. I understand the martyr complex concept all too well. A person with this complex is simply looking for attention. It is all about that person, and his or her thought patterns are selfish. A selfish person is one who simply has his or her priorities wrong.

Instead of being martyrs, God wants us all to be champions. The definition of a champion is "one that does battle for another's rights or honor." Champions are never selfish—that is a strict requirement for champions. They should be willing, even eager, to fight for someone else's rights when necessary. All great champions in the Word knew one thing: It was not about them or their abilities; it was about God and His ability. That attitude made all the difference in their fight because it wasn't them fighting; it was their trusted friend, their God.

There are many stories in the Bible where we see ordinary people doing extraordinary things: Esther, David, Gideon, Moses, Elijah, and the disciples, just to name a few. All of these great men and women had one thing in common: They each had an ongoing relationship with their God, and He had priority in their lives. Because of their intimate relationship with Him, they trusted Him to use them however He saw fit, to be Lord and final authority of their lives.

Today is no different. Everyone is looking for a champion— one who will take up the battle for them, be a friend to the friendless, love the unlovely, and take up the cause for the widows and orphans. God has programmed a champion in each of us. We have the ability to make a difference in people's lives every day. By making our relationship with God our first priority, we find the courage to do the miraculous, to understand the mysterious, and to run the race victoriously. Champions change the world.

Sadly, with every generation that passes without strong teaching and wise leaders, that godly programming is being overwritten with a different worldly programming, a programming that says the only god to be served is the god of self. This new world programming puts "I" on the throne of our lives. The only thought we are concerned with is, *How will this affect me?* Devotion to God and family are considered old-fashioned, I am sad to say, and from this standpoint, we lose sight of our original purpose—we lose the champion God created in us.

We have been sold a lie that says if we don't take care of ourselves, no one will. But the truth is that when we get our priorities straight and put our relationship with God first in our lives, the results are astonishing.

When we lay down our ambitions and our selfish pride and put what God desires above our own agenda, we become an unstoppable force of love and power! When our priorities are right, our focus becomes clear, and our motives and our hearts are clean and pure. There is no better sleep than the sleep of one whose heart is clean.

> Who shall ascend into the hill of the LORD? or who shall stand in his holy place? He that hath clean hands, and a pure heart; who hath not lifted up his soul unto vanity, nor sworn deceitfully. He shall receive the blessing from the LORD, and righteousness from the God of his salvation.
>
> Psalm 24:3–5

Priority #2: SPOUSE

I occasionally watch Dr. Phil, and the times I agree with him most are the times when he says exactly what I am thinking—but he says it with much more wit and humor. I have lost count of the number of couples who come on his show ready to divorce because they have "drifted apart." "Drifted apart" simply means that they no longer have the same interests, they no longer spend time with each other, they no longer have any clue what their spouse is doing or thinking. The key words here are "no longer," which tells us that there was a time when they had the same interests, they spent time together, they knew what their spouse was doing and thinking. What changed? Their priorities changed.

Years ago we attended a function where we met the cutest young newlyweds. She hung onto his every word, he was attentive and considerate, and her eyes said, "Look at this perfect man!" I chuckled, smiled, and then became nauseated because spending just a few minutes with this couple was like spending hours sampling in a candy shop; the sight and smell of all that candy can be overpowering after a while. I was at that point with this couple. I looked for a way to exit the conversation and felt like I needed a good dose of a stomach medicine for my nausea.

Then I realized I wasn't nauseated; I was jealous. I thought to myself, *When did I quit looking at Dennis like that?* I was astonished at my answer: *I never looked at Dennis like that.* When was Dennis attentive and considerate like this young man? I could not come up with an answer.

This couple had something that we never had—they had truly made each other a priority from the beginning of their relationship. The funny thing is that deep down, we all know that to have a truly ideal marriage, you must keep your marriage as a priority and must never take the marriage for granted.

We all know it, but do we do it? Of course not. That is why there are so many divorces today. Knowing to do something and not doing it is called sin.

But this couple, as young as they were, was off to a great start. Somewhere, someone taught them how to be married the right way. Good for them!

How many couples were like us—they didn't start their marriage right? They had no idea what making their spouse a priority meant. Perhaps, like us, they were so messed up when they got married that they didn't know how to make things right. For us, it took years (and we are still learning), but our goal was to have a magnificent marriage—not just for ourselves, but for our children.

Dennis and Linda

After almost thirty years of marriage, Dennis and I have been through every "phase" of marriage. Ironically, the honeymoon months were not my favorite. We were two young (very young) people, and like most young people, we were selfish. Our idea of marriage was so far from God's idea of marriage; we almost divorced in our first year! We both came from fractured homes, so we, too, were fractured. Dennis couldn't remember ever seeing his parents touch each other! Not one hug or kiss, or any outward signs of affection.

Because he had no one to demonstrate what marriage should be, even though he loved me, he struggled when it came to showing any kind of love. I was devastated. I came from a family that at least hugged and kissed one another. Don't get me wrong; my family was just as dysfunctional in many other ways, but we knew how to show (conditional) love—"conditional" being the key word. But when you are young and immature, you think conditional love is love. Beloved, I was messed up!

Loving married couples were supposed to show each other love. Dennis didn't show me that love, so I concluded he didn't love me. What you dwell on in your thought life is where you go in your actions. Since I thought he didn't love me, I acted on those thoughts. I made what was a small problem (easily fixed with counseling) a huge mountain of bitterness, anger, and resentment. In other words, I made matters worse. I grew more bitter and meaner by the day. I often pouted for weeks and gave looks that would make a hateful shrew proud. I know, I know, we were messed up!

Many years into our marriage a dear sister, sis Lee, came to our church and started having small Bible studies in her home. That's when things began to change. It was with her guidance in the Word of God that I truly saw myself for the first time in my life. I was messed up!

That was the beginning of my life. I was on God's operating table without anesthesia, and although the process was often painful, today I am a new woman. Sis Lee became my spiritual mother, my teacher, and my friend. The only charge for her services was the promise that I would duplicate myself in others and make her a spiritual grandmother. It is something I have done over and over with the same conditions that Lee set forth—that my spiritual children go out and duplicate themselves. We must effect change in the next generation, or marriage as God intended will be all but lost.

One of the worst mistakes we make as parents is not understanding that how we conduct our marriage is how our children will conduct their marriages. Right or wrong, good or bad, children's first marriage classes are taught by their parents!

What if every married couple had to commit to going to a marriage class before they could be married? Now, imagine our parents are our marriage teachers, and we are our children's marriage teachers. Well, guess what? That is exactly how life works. Scary thought, huh? It's no surprise when we find ourselves so messed up and start our marriages off with the wrong ideas! That is why there are so many marriages ending in divorce—the teacher and the curriculum desperately need to be revised.

Our young couples are learning the wrong material from the very beginning. Unfortunately, the school of our parents is one school where we cannot skip class because we live in their school daily.

Remember that children are quick learners and don't easily forget what they are taught, especially if it is taught repeatedly. Again, we learn by example, right or wrong.

If we understood that everything we say and do as parents is teaching our children about love, family, marriage, and even finances, maybe we would spend a little more time on our knees and a little less time in front of the television.

As parents, we create the pattern that our children will live by for the rest of their lives. If the parents are selfish, they are not only ruining their marriage, but they are ruining their children's marriages—even the marriages that haven't happened yet. Friend, unless someone gets a clue and changes, this pattern will continue from generation to generation. I heard a story years ago that says it all when it comes to family.

A young woman was getting ready to prepare her first Christmas dinner. As her new husband proudly watched his sweet young bride prepare the Christmas ham, she took a knife and cut off almost a third of the ham!

"What in the world did you do that for?" he asked.

"That is the way my mother did it, and she always made the best ham," she said with a smile.

"But why are you wasting all of that ham?" he pressed.

"It's just the way it must be done to make it like Mom's," she said defensively.

"I don't think you are doing it right," he protested.

"Fine," she huffed. "We will call my mother!"

The call was placed, and the young bride explained the situation to her mother. Her mother agreed that she was doing it right and a huge portion of the ham must be discarded. Still, the young groom protested at such wastefulness.

"Well, that is the way my mother did it," said the bride's mother. "And that is the way I have done it all my life."

Since the young man could not accept that answer, the bride called her grandmother to settle the issue.

"Well," she said slowly, "that is the way my mother did it, and we have been cooking our hams that way ever since I can remember."

"But," the young man persisted, "how does it make the ham better? I really don't understand."

Finally, a decision was reached that the bride's ninety-year-old great-grandmother would be called, and she would once and for all set this young man in his place. This family had been cooking the best hams for generations, and now this know-it-all comes along and questions their cooking methods? The great-grandmother was reached, and her daughter began telling her of the reason for the call.

The bride said, "So, Great-grandma, tell him why we cut one-third of our hams off and why it makes our hams so delicious."

The phone was silent for a few minutes as the elderly woman thought. "Well, I had to cut the ham off. I only had one baking pan, and the ham was always too big for the pan," she said. Every generation had done exactly as the generation before, not knowing why. While this is a very humorous story, it is also dreadfully accurate when it comes to our marriages and our families today.

Let me put it another way. Think of a CD being played continuously in our head—the same songs play day and night, never changing for our entire lives. An infant is born with a blank CD. The CD production starts the day that child comes into this world and ends the day he or she leaves. Everything that baby, infant, toddler, adolescent, and young adult sees, hears, and experiences creates the words and music that are being played minute by minute in his or her head.

That is what happens when we grow up and get married—all of our thoughts and actions are determined by what was previously recorded.

The only way to stop that CD from playing the same toxic thing over and over for the rest of our lives is to change what is on the CD. It can be done. God, in His infinite wisdom, gave us a rewritable CD. We can change it!

But Beloved, it can't be done halfway. This kind of change takes a full commitment. It is not enough to just erase the old poisonous words. All those old words need to be replaced with new, affirming, positive words and actions. This will not happen overnight, and it does not come easy, but a new CD is worth more than all the gold in the world.

So many people are walking around wounded, and they don't know why. Their marriage is in ruins, and they don't know why. They have no hope for happiness in their lives, and again, they don't know why. They can't seem to get it right when it comes to relationships, and they don't know why.

My friend, the *why* is easy if you consider how they have been programmed to think and react over the years. They have had the same thing playing twenty-four seven in their minds for as long as they can remember. It is a fact that where the mind goes, the rest of the person follows.

We have a huge responsibility concerning our child's outlook on marriage, life, and family. But don't despair. God has equipped us for the challenge!

When two people come into a marriage, they are already playing their CDs in their heads. They come into marriage already wounded by their parents' marriage—they just don't realize it. Hurting people hurt people. And when two hurting people get married, it's a dreadful mess.

Dennis and I were just that—we were a dreadful mess. We both had been raised by strong mothers and non-committal fathers. Our contaminated CDs were playing twenty-four seven, and we were following them, spirit, mind, and body. Things were terrible, and we didn't know why.

Dennis's CD was playing a melody of hurt, rejection, isolation, and disappointment. His parents continually distanced themselves from one another and their children. Neither of his parents were believers. His mother had been deeply hurt early in her marriage with Dennis's father, and hurting people hurt people. That is all she knew to do.

Beloved, when a mother is hurting, the whole family is hurting. As women, we need to be whole for the sake of our family. Satan has a specialized attack against women. If Satan can make us feel helpless, hopeless, and worthless and can keep us tired, discouraged, and hanging on to hurt and resentment, then he has our entire family. We can't let that happen. We must be free so that our families will be free.

Because Dennis's mother was bound, he came into our marriage bound by the same things. After all, that is the melody that was playing for him every day of his life.

I came into the marriage with some of the same melody—hurt, rejection, and disappointment—but I also had a bonus reel of insecurity, a song that is on *The Greatest Hits* selection for a lot of women.

It is so important for children to have wonderful role models. I was blessed to have some really great people in my life. For a short time as a child, I spent some wonderful moments with my Great-grandpa and Great-grandma Knight. They were as close to perfect as I have ever known anyone to be. They never raised their voices, their lives were full of peace and contentment, they never spoke poorly of anyone, and they always had a cheerful outlook on life! I still cherish the short time I was with them, and even in those short six to nine years, they made an impact on my life for the better.

Unfortunately, I didn't get to pick how much time I got to spend with these fabulous people. I was quite young, and they were really old. (Of course, now that I am older, they don't seem to have been that old after all!) What time we had was limited, and my attention span was a little on the short side. Nonetheless, even that small window of time we had together is priceless to me as an adult.

And then there was my hero, my dad's mother, Grandma Lorene, who was the daughter of my wonderful Great-grandpa and Great-grandma Knight. Grandma Lorene was practically perfect in my eyes. She was my heart, and even seven years after her death I still mourn for her.

Every child needs, deserves, and must have someone in his or her life who will be stable and loving no matter what is going on around the person, someone who has his or her priorities right and never backs down from doing the right thing. Beloved, that is a champion.

Grandma Lorene was my champion. She never forgot her priorities. She loved God above everything else, and she worked in the church and community all of her (almost) ninety-one years. She taught Sunday school and led the women's group from her church the week she passed away.

Second to her God and her faith was my Grandpa Dwight. No matter how unkindly he treated her with his insufferable negativity, his sullen moods, or his never-ending selfish actions, she always treated him with loving-kindness and respect. She kept a perfect house, never missed having his meals on the table, shared in the farming, took care of the animals, and even did Grandpa's chores when he didn't feel well—which happened with some frequency. While doing all of this, she still had time for her children and grandchildren. We were at her home when we were young—some weeks even more than we were at our own house!

She knew the secret to pure love; she loved unconditionally. Because of her love for my grandpa, she had great peace and suffered from no regrets when he passed away. She always kept him as a priority. Her example of a godly wife, mother, and grandmother still teaches me today. She didn't just talk the talk; she walked the walk. I still mourn the fact that I was too childishly self-centered to pay closer attention to how she did it all and did it so effortlessly. Being selfish robs you of precious time and beautiful relationships.

You would think that since I had such a great role model, my CD would play a better tune. While I had intermittent breakthrough happy songs, right thoughts, and good intentions, like most people, I spent the most time around my parents.

Further deleting anything positive in my life was the fact that we moved away from my grandparents when I was eleven. I was glad that my grandparents wintered with us in Florida, but the time and distance between us the rest of the year proved to be too great a gulf for me to fully recover.

I now see how sad that little girl was—and sadder still were the words she heard daily on her CD. She heard words that affirmed daily that she was never good enough, not pretty, not of great value.

Children should have a symphony of love playing on their CDs. Their songs should shout that they are loved not by one or two individuals, but they are surrounded by people who love them unconditionally twenty-four hours a day, seven days a week! What do you think your thought life would be like if you heard that kind of CD daily in your head?

You know how it is when you get a song in your head and you hum it all day long? My prayer is that every person has a sweet melody playing in his or her heart and soul every day, a melody that says:

> You are loved.
> You are special.
> You can achieve greatness.
> You will be happy.
> You are smart.
> You are talented.
> You are funny.
> You are pretty.
> You are a miracle.

What a great world that would be if each of us plays that CD for everyone around us. If enough people listen to that CD, there will be a new generation of children who marry, stay married, and teach their children to do the same, happily bouncing to their CD of love, praise, and happiness.

Regrettably, my mom's mother shared the same idea that most post-sixties women espoused—that women need something to fall back on just in case something happens to their marriage. Talk about setting the tone and words to your marriage CD early!

So many women of the sixties took up the cry of independence—women relying only on themselves, not depending on their husbands for anything! After she went to work, she and my grandfather separated everything; checkbooks, bank accounts, bedrooms, groceries were all split down the middle. They had turned their marriage into a living arrangement. They fought constantly, and no one won—not them, not their kids, and not their grandkids.

While there is nothing wrong with a woman working outside of the home, remember, we are talking about priorities. We need women in the work force, but more and more, there are too many pressures put on women today to be everything. It is a trap! We need to give ourselves some grace and say, "I am only human. And while I can do all things through God that strengthens me, all things might just not be advantageous for me at this moment in time."

When my youngest brother started school, my mother went to nursing school. The autumn that my mom went to nursing school, our family's lives changed forever. Our home was turned upside down. My mother became independent of her husband, a self-made woman, free from my father's authority financially and otherwise.

Please remember, we are talking about prioritizing our marriages. The example set before me was a damaging one, not because my mom worked. My mom is an intelligent woman and the best OB nurse in the universe. I am sure she did the best job of juggling things she knew how to do at that time. But because when she went to work, she fractured herself from my dad. Fractures need time to heal, but when ignored, they can heal crookedly, leaving a noticeable limp. I never noticed that my grandparents' marriage had the same limp as my parents' did until it was almost too late. Too many times we can look at our parents and know we don't want to end up with a marriage like theirs, but we don't stop and learn why their marriage was so unbearable, so we end up with the same results. Remember the ham? Same thing.

Talk about baggage! Dennis and I were well over the limit allowed by law for a good marriage. We both had learned to look out for ourselves and didn't know how to put anyone before ourselves, especially not our spouse. Yet, like most couples, we got married because we wanted to be married. It was what we wanted, and we knew how to get what we wanted. We had seen the pattern enough. We knew how the game was played. Regrettably, it was not a game.

When reality set in (about a day or so after the wedding), we had to figure out for ourselves that marriage was not a game because it was no fun. We thought we would live happily ever after, but we didn't even know how to live happily on a daily basis. How could two miserable people make each other happy? The answer is they can't. What makes matters worse is that these two miserable souls have children and begin to duplicate their own CD for their children, and the cycle continues.

Beloved, it doesn't have to be that way. The story doesn't have to end sadly. Parents can learn to make one another their priority; they can learn to love and value each other above themselves.

Here is the secret. We have to quit thinking about what we want, need, and desire, and think of what our spouse wants, needs, and desires. We must literally place our spouse's needs and desires above our own.

We all know we should, but we are trained to put ourselves first. If we don't, no one else will, right? Beloved, this is a lie from the pit of hell. It actually works just the opposite. If we put our spouse first, he or she will gladly put us first—really!

Marriage is like a huge ship. You can't turn a huge ship too quickly, or it will sink. It takes finesse and patience to make that huge ocean liner change directions. Our marriage is like that huge ocean liner. It won't completely change directions overnight. It takes patience and great finesse, but it can start that turn in the new direction with an unwavering decision on our part and a fervent commitment to change.

After we have made the decision and commitment, we must take action. No matter how hard the captain wants the ship to change directions, he still needs to take the wheel and turn it in the direction he wants it to go. We can take that wheel, Beloved, and turn that ship around!

Making our spouse a priority is vital for the success of our marriage. Practice makes perfect—well, almost perfect. Remember when the young woman was asked how she got to Carnegie Hall?

She said, "Practice, practice, practice!"

Beloved, the same principle applies to marriage. We all need to practice daily putting our spouses first. Practice daily erasing that old CD of hurt and confusion. Practice daily filling our minds and our souls with sweet words of love and redemption.

The decisions we make about our marriages today will be tested and tried, but the rewards far exceed the temporal inconveniences we will experience. There is nothing more gratifying than knowing that the time we spend making our marriage a success is really time we spend making our children's marriages successful as well.

Many years ago, my mom did a lot of sewing. She was an expert seamstress. She would go to the fabric store and buy a pattern for whatever it was she wanted to make and then have the brilliance to follow that pattern perfectly. Although the print and color of the fabric varied, everything she made off of the same pattern looked the same as the garment before it. Marriages are much like a pattern. When we have an excellent pattern, every garment will be just as wonderful as the garment before it. We owe it to the future generations to cut and sew the fabric of our marriages with great care. Soon enough, our dear children will use that very same pattern for their marriages as well.

Irreconcilable Differences

Irreconcilable differences are the hinge pin of many divorces. Have we ever stopped to ask ourselves, "What are irreconcilable differences?" According to the dictionary, "irreconcilable differences" means "not able to reconcile." In other words, "not able to restore, resolve, or settle their differences."

Many times, we hear a couple is marrying, and we might think they are making a huge mistake. We may even be so bold as to share our concerns with the couple or perhaps individually, and yet the couple feels compelled to get married despite the evidence that is mounted against them on the side of caution. Quite often, this points to immaturity on the part of the engaged couple. And while immaturity is a major problem in marriages today, it is one that usually gives way to wisdom as the couple gets older and more mature in the Lord and in age. There is a far more serious problem in marriages than immaturity. That old enemy we talked about previously causes the most heartache—selfishness.

Consider the couple who have been married for several years. Let's say, for argument's sake, that they married when the young woman was very young and very much in love with her husband. In this scenario, they have a couple of children and settle into a happy suburban life. The unfortunate part comes when the bride ages and this older woman feels that life has passed her by. She is convinced that she has missed out on the best years of her life.

This lie from the enemy comes at first in small whispers. She seems to encounter, with some frequency, people she has known for years who divorced and began dating again. They are doing things that this young wife and mother only dreamed of doing. She begins to see her husband and her children as a heavy noose tightening forcefully around her neck, each day sucking the very life out of her. Beloved, this is what she sees because this is what she chooses to see. When we are enticed by the enemy, we choose to think his ways, see things his way, and eventually even say what he is saying. Sorrowfully, the enemy wins when we are tempted and led away from the plans of the Father and into a life of compromise and sin.

In our scenario, the woman begins to look for excuses to leave her marriage and live what she has decided will be a much happier, fun-filled life of single bliss. Because we are all flesh, if we look hard enough at our spouse, we are sure to find a huge boulder of offense teetering on the edge of discovery that we have long over-looked—a boulder that, when given the right amount of pressure at just the right time, will come rumbling down the side of the old dangerous cliff of mistrust and indifference. This misguided woman capitalizes on her husband's shortcomings and begins to use them as weapons to chisel away at her once happy home.

The woman we imagine here has been lied to and deceived by the enemy, but she can't see that. She only sees what, in her estimation, is best for her. Neither her husband nor her children carry any weight in her decision. My friend, when the enemy comes to tempt, he only has a few weapons in his arsenal. The problem is that we fall for them every time. That is why he can keep using them against us. In this case, he uses the woman's lust for a more exciting life to deceitfully blind her to what she is truthfully giving up and what she is ultimately gaining.

My sister, the devil can NEVER tell the whole truth. There might be some glimmer of truth in what he is whispering, but it is never the whole truth. In this story, the woman leaves her husband and takes the children on a winding journey of sadness as she goes from one man to another trying to find the happiness she deserves. Each stop on her journey makes another groove in the CD that her children will one day replay. Songs filled with hopelessness, selfishness, sadness, loneliness, and deceit. Sadly, while she digs herself deeper and deeper into a life of sin and shame to seek that illusive gratification, she buries her family in the ditch right along with her.

Our tired, life-worn woman is left twenty years later with only the "what-ifs." What if she had chosen to stay and weather out the storms of her emotions in the marriage? What if she had stopped the enemy when he whispered the first of many lies he would use against her and her marriage? What if she had turned her selfishness into selflessness toward her husband?

Her choices had been made, and her fate, without repentance, was sadly sealed. She can't turn back the hands of time. Her husband had long since moved on and made a life for himself without her. Her children, who were once happy and carefree, lost in a world of dress-up and make-believe, are now lost to a world of sin, taken captive by the same enemy that had captured their mother.

When we follow our flesh, living a life only for our self-gratification, and forget the principle of priority, we are not the only casualties. Everyone who is involved in our lives gets wounded somehow or another. Remember, hurting people hurt people, and without change, the cycle continues from generation to generation.

Irreconcilable differences are only irreconcilable if we refuse to restore our marriage, resolve our problems, and settle our differences. It is ultimately our own choice.

Just because we are tired of being married, that is not an excuse for a divorce. Every marriage will go through a time of complacency, or what some term a "rut." It is up to us to take an interest in our marriage. If we are not interested in our own marriage, who will be? So many of us sob that we don't have anything in common or we just don't get along with our spouses. My sister, these temporal situations are not excuses for a divorce. They are, however, screaming cues that we need to wake up, roll up our sleeves, and get to work on making our marriages better. Beloved, marriage is work, but it is worth every moment we invest in it.

Sorrowfully, in this society, getting a divorce is easier than working on our marriages. A successful marriage, like a successful garden, needs constant weeding and watering every day in order to keep it giving its maximum yield.

My grandma used to have a huge garden. Early in the morning, while it was still cool, Grandma was on her knees pulling weeds and carefully examining every plant. She made sure no critters were nibbling on her greens and no creepy-crawly was getting fat off of her berries. It was her garden, and she tended it daily. She was still tending that garden at eighty-eight years old. Beloved, if an almost ninety-year-old woman can weather heat, critters, and the physical agony of a quarter-acre plot of ground to supply her family with the best food, then I truly believe we can have that same tenacity when it comes to taking care of our spouses and protecting our marriages.

I chuckle when a married woman looks at another woman's husband and wishfully thinks he is fair game. *Honey,* I think to myself, *the reason that husband looks so good is because someone is weeding and watering that garden.* Grass is only greener on the other side because someone else is doing the watering. If we take care of our own gardens, we won't have the time to worry about what is going on in someone else's.

The reason for this chapter is to keep us from the pain and agony that divorce causes. No one wins when it comes to a divorce. The stories of infidelity and betrayal in marriages are endless. In every case, without exception, the offending spouse is led astray by the lust of his or her own flesh. Meanwhile, the person's entire family is destroyed in the aftermath.

Not everyone is a willing participant in divorce. But it is true that some divorces happen because two people have forgotten to put each other first, let other things take priority over their marriage, or become numb to each other's needs. These marriages cannot be saved until the couple changes their priorities. There are instances, however, where one of those two people tries desperately to save and resurrect their marriage, and the other spouse will not make any effort at all. They are willing, even eager, for it to fail—much like the young woman in our previous story. This leaves one spouse abandoned and broken. If this has happened to you, I am sincerely sorry. My heart goes out to those spouses who have been discounted and discarded. If that is you, please know that the Father loves you and knows your pain; His thoughts toward you are good. You will overcome this evil that has been done to you. Take refuge in the Savior and in close friends. God is a God of tomorrows, and He has planned a great one for you!

I cannot leave the topic of the pillar of priority with our spouse without hitting on the common problems in most marriages. These small problems are little cracks, easily fixed. Picture, if you will, the difference between filling in a crack in our driveway and filling in the Grand Canyon. I know which one I would rather fill! This is what happens to marriages. People don't just drift apart; they make a choice to be apart. But what do we do when these little cracks become big gaping crevices in our marriage and little problems become irreconcilable differences?

Time, Money, and Sex

When it comes to the finances in a marriage, the only—and I repeat, the only—godly approach is the ours/ours approach. (That is the opposite of the yours/mine approach.) If two people work, the money they earn should go into a joint account for mutually agreed upon expenditures. If only one spouse works, the same principle applies. Marriage in its definition is the act of being joined, a union, two people becoming one entity. When we take any part of that union and split it, whether it is finances, sex, even entertainment, you are forming cracks in the foundation that will lead to wide crevices, which now take an even greater effort to repair.

Another small crack comes in the marriage when two people spend too much time apart. We ought to not continuously choose to do things that we know our spouse doesn't want to participate in and go places where our spouse doesn't want to go. For instance, when choosing a movie, we should not disregard our spouse's likes and always choose the movie we want to see. I don't particularly like action/adventure movies, but Dennis does. So I go to whatever movie he wants to see. I tell him to keep the popcorn coming, and I can sit through any action film! That, Beloved, is called compromise. A successful marriage is full of agreeable compromises.

And while there is nothing wrong with a woman going to the mall without her husband, if we went to the mall every night without our husbands, we would be creating a very deep (not to mention, expensive) crevice.

I cannot tell you the number of husbands who feel ignored because their wife stays on the phone all night. Beloved, if our husband is home, we should not ignore him by spending our precious time talking to someone else. We must learn to be considerate. I remember the first time Dennis came home and I was on the phone, and I said, "Oh, I need to go. Dennis is home." I thought he was going to pass out from amazement. That went a long way that night. He gave me attention that evening that he hadn't in a long time just because I had showed him the respect he was due as my husband.

Now, what if our husband is in the middle of a four-hour football game? We can take advantage of the time and be on the phone a little, but we should take a breather every now and then to see how his favorite team is doing. Be interested! A little kindness goes a long way in a marriage.

Turning off the television when our spouse wants to talk will show our spouse he or she is a priority. Look him or her in the eyes; really listen. That will tell your spouse he or she is loved, and your spouse will respond in like manner—really!

Sex is not just a physical activity; it is spiritual as well. God makes us one with our spouses through intimacy and spending that close time together. Remember, God—not humans—invented sex. God knew what He was doing, and He did it well. When it comes to sex, making time to spend together is a priority.

But to take advantage of this wonderful intimacy, we must be present in the same room at the same time. We can't live separate lives and have a healthy sex life. We also can't watch TV all night and have a healthy sex life. We must make ourselves available to each other if we are to have the intimacy that God intended us to have.

If we have to plan a time to be together, we need to do it. If we have to get away for a weekend to rekindle the passion we once had, then we need to do it. When it comes to sex, we need to make intimacy with our spouses high on our list. The subject of sex can be one of the greatest sources of stress in a marriage. We must not let the enemy get a foothold when it comes to the intimacy we share with our spouses. We need to talk to our spouses about our sexual relationships. Communication is the key to a good sexual relationships. The marriage bed is the last place we need to be selfish. Intimacy is a two-way street. When we make the decision to keep our spouses and our marriages a priority in our lives, we will keep those cracks of monotony and discontent from forming and becoming a sinkhole of frustration that will soon explode into a canyon on the verge of a divorce.

Keeping our spouses as a priority isn't easy, especially when children come, but it can and must be done. When our children are young, we can't fathom not having all the harried excitement that children bring into our lives, but believe me, it will happen. Soon enough, we will be alone again, and our children will be grown, gone, and leading lives of their own.

Beloved, it is essential that we cultivate our time together as a loving couple while we still have children. We cannot afford to wait until we are finally alone. By then, we will be too far apart. We must practice our pillar of priority continuously when it comes to our spouses so when the time comes and our children are grown and gone, we won't have the empty nest syndrome; we'll have the "hallelujah" syndrome!

There is nothing more precious than a couple of lovebirds who have been married forty, fifty, or sixty years still holding hands, snuggling up to each other in the movies, or sharing a smile for reasons only the two of them know. Beloved, that should be one of our greatest goals—to live, love, laugh, and enjoy our spouse and our marriages all the days of our lives! As with doing anything that is right, there is a benefit that comes with making our spouses a priority; we automatically give our children a head start in their own race of life. Through our example, our children can know that a great marriage can be theirs, and with the blueprint right in front of them, they only need to follow it in order to have a successful marriage themselves.

Priority #3: CHILDREN

When did being an attentive mom become such a bad thing? When did it become socially unacceptable to be the best wife and mother we could be? Why does society set such little value on a woman who places value on her family? Think about it. A forty-hour-per-week job is considered full time. Yet, we expect to have a full-time career and simultaneously devote ourselves to raising successful children.

The same thing goes for fathers. When did it become acceptable for a father to work eighty hours a week? When did it become the right thing for fathers to spend all their extra time on the weekends playing golf, watching sports, or being with friends and doing hobbies, and spend no time with their families?

When did it become a normal occurrence for a man to have children with one woman, leave, go out, and have children with another woman, and then ignore all of them? When did it become acceptable for women to have children by multiple men and not stay married to one of them? Husbands need their wives, wives need their husbands, and children need their parents.

We need to examine our priorities when it comes to our children and not pay attention to what the world deems acceptable or unacceptable. Many families are falling apart, and children are left parenting themselves (poorly). Parents have the right and responsibility to parent children in a godly manner and not care who approves or disapproves.

I tried several times to work outside our home while raising four sons. I was cranky, my house was a mess, and my husband and I fought constantly. I quit the same position four times. God bless the man who kept hiring me. He hired me because, as a Christian, I gave the position 110 percent, I loved to learn, and I was eager to do my job to the best of my ability. My boss made several exceptions for me. He even let me pick up my children after school and take them back to the office for an hour and a half when our babysitting situation fell through. With these and many more exceptions that he made for me, I still could not balance my work, my home life, and family.

I know there are millions of godly women who do balance work, family, marriage, and everything else with success. Sadly, I was not one of those women. God bless all of the working mothers who are juggling both while having babies and small children at home. I truly believe it takes a special person to do all of these things at the same time. But I do believe that in doing all of these things at the same time, something or someone gets left out. Many times, it is the woman herself who gets left out. Other times, it is the marriage, and in many cases, it is the children.

After all my children were raised, I began working again. This time I only needed to balance my marriage, grown kids, church, and work. This was a piece of cake compared to what I had to do years earlier. I am not saying it was super easy, but compared to what I was up against before, I at least had time to breathe and keep my house in order.

> A wise man's heart discerneth both time and judgment.
> Ecclesiastes 8:5b

I had to learn what timing was best for me and judge it for myself when it came to my family and working outside of the home. This is something that every couple must do for themselves.

One of the greatest fallacies that is rampant among parents today is that when children reach thirteen, they are raised and no longer need their parents to be home with them. Beloved, that is so far from the truth, it is fiction! I read an article years ago that said more than 80 percent of the girls who were pregnant and under the age of eighteen became pregnant while having sex in their own beds while both parents were at work! If anything, teenagers need more parental involvement than babies do. Babies eat, sleep, cry, and poop, and while our presence is important, they spend most of their time occupying themselves.

Teenagers, on the other hand, are at an awkward time when they are making so many life-changing decisions—who their friends are, where to spend their time, where to cruise on the Internet, what to watch on TV, what to see at the movies, as well as decisions related to driving, eating, drinking, smoking, drugs, sex, their future. Does this sound like something that they need to do on their own? All of these areas of a teenager's life cry out for parental wisdom—wisdom that comes from being there, doing that, wisdom that comes from keeping God as your first priority, wisdom that comes from knowing exactly what is going on in our own homes.

Frankly, many parents today don't know what is going on under their own roofs! Reports tell of kids doing things that are considered undesirable, maybe even illegal, in their parents' homes. With so much going on in their own lives today, too many parents are alarmingly oblivious to what is happening right under their own noses.

A parent's job is to be ever vigilant. We will answer one day to God for what we did with the most precious gift He had to give us—His children. Beloved, we will have to give an answer, and it must be, as with all things of the Father, a truthful answer. What will we say?

Children don't raise themselves. They can't. They don't have the resources, experience, maturity, or wisdom. These are the resources that parents are supposed to have and use on a daily basis. What happens when the parents are so preoccupied with their own lives that the children take last place?

Let's go over our priorities:

#1: God

#2: Spouse

#3: Children ... that would be third place, correct?

Children are not a thing we do after work or something we try to get to on the weekends. Children are not the priority after I go out or after my friends and I have had a great time. Children are our priority.

Let me give a word of caution. Making your child or children your priority does not mean you must give them everything they could possibly want or need. The stress put on parents today to give their children everything is simply the work of the enemy. He knows if he can keep the parents working themselves to a frazzle to give their children everything under the sun, the parents will have no time for God, their marriage, or their children.

Have you ever noticed that parents who work so hard so their children can "have it all" have the toughest time raising successful children? The mothers and fathers who work overtime so that each of their children can have their own televisions, cable boxes (even the toddlers), and, of course, their own game systems rarely spend time with their spouse or children.

We are not talking about the single parent here who has to work to provide food and shelter for the children. Nor are we talking about couples who have to scrimp on everything they can and are still forced to both work to provide the basic needs of their families.

We are talking about feeding our children to the idols of greed and lust. We are talking about parents putting their children in preschool before dawn and picking them up after dark so that the parents can live a luxurious lifestyle. Sadly, these children often act out because they cannot express their grief over being apart from their parents all of their waking hours. Unfortunately, the parents don't notice because they are working eighty hours a week and are too exhausted to deal with the children on the weekends. In some cases, that's why parents buy their children all those things—to keep them busy so the parents won't have to be involved.

Fighting among preschool children is on the rise, as is abuse toward their teachers and those in authority. Why do you think these children are so angry? Is it because they do not have enough stuff at home to play with? I think not.

The parents we are talking about will tell you they are working for their families, but if the truth be told, many times, they are actually working for their own self-worth and self-gratification. They want what they want, and nothing will stand in their way of getting it—especially not their children.

We all know families like I have described. The children are often out of control at home, and at school, they either turn inward and become loners or search desperately for someone, anyone, to love them and pay them a little attention. Either scenario can be a dangerous one.

Many times, the parents have several children, and the care for all the children is put on the older child. All too often, an older child will have great responsibility thrust on him or her at an early age. Children should get to be children while they are young, and they should not be forced to take on adult responsibilities too soon; the results could be disastrous.

While I was in a store a few months back, there was a missing child alert. Everyone was searching frantically for the small child who had vanished. Like most other shoppers, we took up the search. A couple of minutes into the search, I came across a young girl about eight years old, crying. Triumphantly, I found a store employee and announced I had found the young child. I was shocked to learn from the store clerk that this young girl was not the missing child; she was the sister of the missing child who was watching her while the mother shopped. This child was inconsolable. She heaved with sobs while searching for her young sister. My heart went out to her. What a horrible position to put a child in—she was too young for such responsibility. After about fifteen minutes, the missing child was found hiding under some clothes. She had a wonderful time playing hide and seek and was mystified at everyone's reaction to finding her. While the story has a happy ending for the missing child, the sister, on the other hand, was being horribly berated by the mother as we left for not keeping a better eye on her young sister. The mother bore no responsibility at all in the events of the day.

This, my beloved, is so sad. Parents can become so busy with their own lives that they give the responsibility of their children to anyone who will take it, even another child. God, in His wisdom, gave us these beautiful children. He gave them to us—not to our neighbor, our school system, or our parents, but to us. They are our responsibility to raise. They don't need stuff; they need parents. They don't need activities to keep them busy, they need role models to teach them how to live.

To help us understand the importance of establishing the pillar of priorities, I want to relate a true story to you about a young single mother that I'll call Sara. Sara went through a bitter divorce, but took her children—ages eight, six, and four—to church with her every Sunday. While the children behaved quite well in church, Sara confessed to her church elders that they were practically running over her at home. Sara sought counseling for her four-year-old's unusual behavior:

- He had found the digital camera and was taking pictures of his private areas.
- He was carrying a Victoria's Secret catalog with him around the house.
- He liked to go to restaurants based on the size of the women's breasts.
- He was using foul language and hitting his siblings.
- One day, he went toward the kitchen drawers where the knives were stored and was threatening to kill his brother, sister, and mother.

Whether out of amusement or nervousness, Sara laughed about her youngest child's behavior. She reported that her other two children were yelling at her and each other, constantly fighting and hitting one another, and refused to follow any rules she set in the home. They did not have a bedtime, and when they did go to bed, they all slept in the same bed with their mother, refusing to sleep in their own rooms.

The church elders were surprised to learn that, even though Sara submitted to counseling, she wasn't quite ready to work on getting her home back in order. Sara concentrated more on her personal happiness. Even with all of the stories she told about her children, the longest and saddest story, according to Sara, was her own loneliness. She said she was tired of taking care of the kids while their dad was free to live with his new woman. Sara told the elders what she wanted, and unfortunately, she did not share one thing about what the children wanted or ask for help as to why the children were acting out and putting themselves in danger. Her children were paying a high price for her lack of happiness.

The elders counseled Sara that God should be her first focus, and because she did not have a spouse, her second focus should be her children. Sara didn't want to hear that—she had her eye on a man at church and was trying desperately to get his attention. The elders cautioned her about this man and told her under no circumstances was he a family man. They urged her to put dating on the back burner and make God and then her children her main priorities.

She started dating the man at church that she'd been warned about. He soon moved in with her, and the problems with the children escalated. In a selfish attempt to meet her own needs, Sara lost more than a relationship; the man she pursued eventually cost her thousands of dollars, ruined her credit, and refused to leave her home.

Months later, after this man finally left her home, Sara once again had the opportunity to right her situation and prioritize her life. Instead, Sara moved another man in with her and her children. Her ex-husband got remarried, and the children were shuttled between the two homes, neither of which has them on the priority radar. The parents, with their new relationships, became even more selfish, and the children were shoved further and further down the "to do" list.

One day soon, these children will grow up and start their own relationships. Apart from God's intervention, they will continue the book on parenting that their parents started writing years before, and it will be filled with rejection, anger, bitterness, hopelessness, and fear. If you are a single mom, I urge you—make your children a priority.

This young mother was going through what so many single parents and couples are facing today—they are not being taught how to parent. Too many young parents today don't have anyone to speak into their lives and share life lessons of child rearing. Again, too many parents are over-stressed when it comes to parenting and what is truly expected of them. You can't fix what you don't know to fix. All too often, parents will ignore behavior they don't understand or don't know how to deal with until the problem is so big they can't deal with it.

Many times the fiercest problem facing young families is that the children have all the control. This usually happens early on when the parents let the children have a say in every little thing that goes on in the family. Some examples of parents giving their children too much input might be what to have for dinner, what kind of car the family should drive, where the family eats out, what kind of pet the family might buy, where the family attends church, or where they go on vacation.

When the child has that kind of power, it can go to their heads! It is easy to spot a household where the child or children call the shots. The parents are the followers, and the children are the leaders.

Dennis and I went to a home one evening for dinner. When we arrived, the relative commented that we would eat as soon as the husband came home. He was at a local fast food restaurant getting the youngest child some food. When we looked a little puzzled, the woman explained that the child would only eat a certain kid's meal for dinner, so every night the mother would fix a meal for the rest of the family and then the father would go out and buy a kid's meal for the child. Who do you think was running that home?

When children have control of a home, they say when they eat, what they wear, where they go, what they do, and when they sleep.

If God thought children had the capacity to live on their own, he would have made them like the animals—we would wean them and leave them. But children don't have that capacity. They don't know what is best for them. Determining their best interests is the parents' job. All too often the parents just plain don't want to fight with their child, so they give in. Beloved, we should never fight with our children. There are times things may be discussed, and then there are times we, as parents, should make a decision based on what is best, not only for our children, but the family as a whole. When I was young, we ate what was served, and we were blessed to have it. Today, a mother may cook five different entrees for her family to suit everyone's tastes. This is a mother who is causing stress on herself! Although I didn't think it possible, I never died from eating my vegetables.

I saw a commercial the other day of ravioli that contained a serving of vegetables. The mother didn't want the father to say it out loud, so the child didn't know they were eating their vegetables. While this seems a light thing, again, we are placating this generation. In the commercial, the motivation of the mother seemed to be fear that if the child knew he was eating vegetables, he would stop eating. What are we doing?

Children feel safe when given boundaries and not left to wander willy-nilly. It is our responsibility as parents to give our children those boundaries. We are not bad when we don't let our children make their own choices all the time. We are doing what we were called to do—parent. While there is nothing wrong with letting our children have a choice once in a while, they must know they are not in charge of the home or, for that matter, in charge of themselves. They are our responsibility, and we must do what is best for them, vegetables and all.

A Word to the Servants

Working in and for any ministry can be a great blessing, and the call of God on one's life is a treasured and precious gift that should be taken very seriously. Having said that, it is clear that God does not intend for the call He has placed on our lives to be to the detriment of the family that He ordained from the beginning. He would not have said, "Go forth and multiply" if He hadn't intended for us to take care of the products of that multi-plication; namely, our children. I can find nowhere in the Word where it says we are to sacrifice our children for the kingdom of God. Careers and outside interests can be a huge distraction for parents. So it goes without saying that clergy and lay ministers are also not immune to this temptation.

I have known many pastors and lay ministers in my life who truly love God and have an endless open and giving heart for their congregation and the people of their community. Many times, the pastor is busy in the early years building the church and busier in the later years keeping up with the growth of the church. His wife is usually overworked and underappreciated, trying to be all things to all people in the congregation.

But we are talking about priorities, and the priority of raising our children does not change according to the occupation or anointing on one's life. Church is not an excuse for neglecting our family. Business is not an excuse for neglecting our family. Good causes aren't worth our family members' lives. There is no excuse for neglecting our children. None.

> Fathers, do not irritate and provoke your children to anger [do not exasperate them to resentment], but rear them [tenderly] in the training and discipline and the counsel and admonition of the Lord.
>
> Ephesians 6:4 AMP

Resentment is a strong chain to break no matter what our age. If given a chance to grow, it becomes an even stronger chain controlled by nasty monsters of envy, self-pity, hatred, strife, bitterness, and jealousy. We must render these monsters power-less, and their chains must be broken. All of this can be done while leaning on the pillar of priority.

We all know pastors' kids (PKs) who are suffering. There are so many who are/were competing with sometimes hundreds or thousands of people for their parents' attention. Children (and adults) will go to great lengths to get their parents' attention. No matter how they can get it, in a bad or good way, attention is still attention to a child, and they are willing to do almost anything to get it from their parents.

A pastor will pour his heart and soul into the ministry while his children are hurting and vulnerable to the lies of the enemy. Without teaching and proper parenting, children will do the best they can do, but remember, they don't have the wisdom to make those all-important life decisions alone. Most of the time, chil-dren make poor life choices when left to their own devices.

I personally know many PKs who have left the faith altogether. Their stories are almost always identical. The people of the church were too hard on them, or the people of the church took up too much of their parents' time, and they are so resentful, they can't see past the hurt and get back into fellowship with the church.

What happens when these precious souls are ignored at the cost of the kingdom? Too often, those lost souls have not lost interest in God, but they have lost faith in Him. So much of what they experienced did not line up with the Word they were taught.

The problem usually is that these children know too much of what is really going on in and behind the scenes of church. Too much of the wrong knowledge will lead to cynicism not only of the church, but of God. They begin to doubt everything and everyone—their parents, their faith, and their God. This is when the enemy swoops in to offer the counterfeit, and these wounded babes cannot tell the difference between the real and the fake. After all, what they have seen so many years seems to be a façade, anyway. Who's to say what is real?

What if that is your child? What can be done? First and foremost, we must pray for their restoration to God. Then we need only ask for guidance, and God will lead us into the right direction. We must own our own role in the matter and start from there. Boundaries need to be made, and lines need to be drawn. We must make our children know their value—not only to us, but to God.

I talked to a young pastor recently. He admitted that he was exhausted and his wife and children recently complained about the time the people of the church were taking. It took me all of five minutes to give my precious brother a tutorial on the church, boundaries, and priorities.

Caller ID is there to be used—it is a gift from God. Screen your calls, friends. We all know the ones that can wait and the ones that are urgent. Just because the phone rings doesn't mean it must be answered!

These days we are almost bound by our own cell phones. A pastor need not give his cell number out to the entire church.

He is not obligated to do so, no matter what people might say. I heard of one pastor that has three cell phones—one for his church leaders, one for his close friends and family, and one that is just for his wife and children. Now, that is a pastor who knows how to prioritize!

What about sister Sally, who keeps calling morning, noon, and night? Sis Sally is probably lonely. Find her a buddy, a sister in the Lord, to occupy some of her time. It might be a blessing all the way around.

Cells or group meetings are a good way to delegate the workload of the pastor. As with anything, it is always good to bathe this idea in prayer.

Teams or committees are also a great idea for a pastor. A hospital team can do follow-up visits when a parishioner is sick. A financial team can deal with the people of the church who come with financial needs. This also helps keep the pastor in a pastoral position, not taking on the title of a banker. The list is endless; we must just take the time to get the teams in place and start setting those boundaries for the people around us. Once the boundaries are set and firmly adhered to, most people will obey them.

Everyone needs some downtime. We have some friends who are retired pastors who said one of the biggest mistakes they made when they were young pastors was not taking vacations. Now they are assistant pastors and take three or four vacations a year!

People will wear you out! We all need to take some time to refuel and get ready for what God has for us down the road. Here again, it is hard to hear from God when we are too stressed. Being exhausted does not make us a hero. It makes us unusable in the kingdom.

I can remember the time we were pastoring the children at our local church and we needed a vacation desperately. We didn't have anyone to take our place and felt trapped. Looking back now, I can think of several people who would have filled in for us if we'd asked, but we never asked. There is usually help out there if we would only ask. Beloved, we *have* not because we *ask* not.

We need people around us to take up the slack. For pastors, that person could be the assistant pastor, the deacons, or the lay ministers. If you're a ministry worker and don't have a regular helper or replacement, seek out a friend in your congregation who can be trusted to take over some of your church or ministry duties.

Prioritizing our children means setting aside regular family time, one night of the week that is strictly for the family. This night is non-negotiable. Unless there is a death or someone is dying, we will spend that night together. Even if we just eat dinner together and watch TV, we are still together.

We need to be in constant communication with our children. We need to know what is going on in their hearts and their lives. We need them to know we are there for them, and not just on family night, but every time they need us. Sis Sally can wait once in a while. The phone can even be turned off once in a while (gasp!), and we don't have to talk to every person after church who is demanding our time and attention.

How often is the pastor the first one to the church and the last one out of the church? We are not doing our children a favor when they get to bed too late or miss out on their naps because we have church functions. As much as we love to fellowship on Sundays, we make it a point to not hang around church and talk. Our grandchildren are usually with us, and they need to have lunch and take a nap shortly after church is over. I make no apologies. Our children are our priority. We have made our boundaries firm and have no problem getting them home at a decent time.

My favorite movie of all time is *It's a Wonderful Life*. I love the scene where young George needs to talk to his father. George knows his father is in the middle of a meeting, but rushes in to speak to him anyway. Our children should know they have that kind of access to us. After all, we have that kind of access to our heavenly Father, don't we? How can we want that with Him, and yet deny it to our children?

Even though I am a pastor, I have no desire to pastor a church. I am one of those people who have seen too much and know too much. More of my friends are pastors than are not, so I know all too well the plight of today's shepherds. The church can be a cruel place. But it doesn't have to be. Sheep just need to be trained to be obedient. Fences make good neighbors, and boundaries make good parishioners and good friends.

We can never go wrong making our children a priority. Our children don't care what we do, where we go, or what possessions we have. They do care about how much time we spend with them and how involved we are in their lives. When a father is on his deathbed, he never laments the time he could have spent at work.

He does, however, lament the time he could have spent with his children.

Following the pillar of priority will bring us great peace when our children are older. Our adult children won't be difficult to get along with or easily offended and resentful. They will be happy and full of peace, a peace that comes from knowing your boundaries and knowing you have a secure place in the family, a place of love and acceptance no matter what the situation.

When we prioritize our children, our relationship with them will blossom throughout their adulthood, and they will know, as in their childhood, that they are still a priority.

Let's turn off our TVs, turn on our answering machines, and get off the couch. Our children are only young once, and we won't get a second chance at their childhood. We want them to say when they are older, "My parents made me a priority, and I know I am loved."

The Second Pillar

The Pillar of Consistency

Every good gift and every perfect gift is from above, and cometh down from the Father of lights, with whom is no variableness, neither shadow of turning.

James 1:17

Jesus Christ the same yesterday, and to day, and for ever.

Hebrews 13:8

Both of these Scriptures say the same thing—that God doesn't change, and He is steady. That is why we can depend on Him. I love the fact that I know God is always just a breath away. He doesn't take a vacation, and His answer is always the same—yes and amen.

The reason we keep our faith, no matter what the circumstances say, is that we believe God's Word and know His Word is always the same day after day. It is that consistency that gives us hope for the future. The song "I Don't Know About Tomorrow," by Kelly Price, speaks about knowing that it is Jesus who holds our hand.* It is that blessed assurance that gives us abiding peace. Since God is our Teacher and our Model of parenting, then we, too, should be consistent with our own children. They deserve to know the peace that a deep abiding trust brings.

According to Merriam-Webster's dictionary,** the definition of "consistent" is "marked by harmony, regularity, or steady continuity: free from variation or contradiction."

What a perfect picture these words paint...regularity and harmony, free from contradiction. When I picture a family that has harmony, I see a family that lives in peace. Children who know this kind of peace are rested in their spirit and ready to meet any and all things that may come their way. We will never have peace or rest without consistency.

Children need that consistent stability to feel safe. They need to know that things are going to be the same day after day when it

---

*"I Don't Know About Tomorrow" by Kelly Price
** Merriam-Webster's online dictionary, www.merriam-webster.com

comes to their surroundings. Children need to know they can rely on their parents. They need to know their parents are steadfast and consistent—a rock that will not be moved no matter what happens. Unfortunately, too many parents are more like quicksand, changing with every passing day, never standing firm on any decision, apt at any moment to collapse like an old abandoned building because of their instability.

Because consistency is the foundation that successful parenting is based on, there is a method of instituting consistency, and there are consequences to parenting without it. Consistency begins at childbirth and never ends. Parents today are sometimes so busy with their own lives and what is going on in their own hectic schedule that they don't have the time or energy to deal with one more thing, much less their child's disobedient behavior. It's tempting when we're busy to ignore bad behavior. Beloved, I say this with all gravity and somberness: We either choose to be consistent in dealing with the bad behavior now, or we will deal with much more serious problems later.

Children are not automatically obedient and well-mannered. Weary parents who have an out-of-control three-year-old have no consistency. They think things will eventually get better by simply ignoring the behavior, as if it will miraculously go away, and one day out of the blue, the child will be obedient and well-behaved.

Let me give you a picture of ignoring a behavior. Let's say you have a puppy that is not potty-trained. Can we adopt the attitude that we can just ignore the problem, and the puppy will fully potty train himself? Of course not. The puppy can only be trained if we patiently teach and train it.

The same is true of children. Ignoring a behavior will not make it go away. It will, however, firmly root the child in that bad behavior, getting worse with time. So many parents, young and old, excuse their child's bad behavior with a complacent comment like, "Oh, it will go away if we ignore it. They are only doing it for attention."

My response is (and will always be) the same. What a child is at three he will be at thirteen. A child who throws temper tantrums at three will throw uncontrollable tantrums at thirteen. A child who controls his home at three will be in total command of that same home at thirteen. A child who rebels at three will be in complete rebellion at thirteen.

A child who demands her own way at three will violently demand her own way at thirteen. A child who is allowed to hit his parents at three will abuse his parents at thirteen. A child who defies a parent at three will treat that same parent with contempt at thirteen.

Beloved, don't despair. Any damage already done can be repaired—with consistency. Whether your child is three or twenty-three, consistency is the key to a peaceful home.

Consistency works for good and for bad. One Sunday, I was teaching a children's class, and I was using an object lesson about listening to parents and giving proper respect when they say no. A child in the back, who had been a real challenge in the beginning, raised his hand and said, "Pastor Linda, if I keep asking and asking and asking, I always get what I want." Of course, I had to tell him that just because he got what he wanted from his parents, that didn't make it right. But he was a smart child and had it figured out. All he had to do was keep asking, and his parents caved in. They had proved to him they were consistent. They were consistently giving in to his inappropriate behavior.

As my husband and I discussed this incident later, everything we had seen in this family became crystal clear. The disrespect the children had for their parents, the trouble in the parents' marriage all pointed to a lack of priorities, and inconsistencies in their lives. Children are smart. They learn how their parents tick early on. They know the buttons to push and how far they can go, all because they have learned that their parents are always consistent.

Whether we know it or not, we are consistent parents. The question is, What kind of consistency are we displaying? Either we consistently discipline and reward our children, keeping ever vigilant, or we consistently ignore our children, unaware of what is happening in our own home. Perhaps we are spending too many hours concentrating on our own life and our own affairs instead of investigating what is going on in our children's lives and their affairs. Sounds a little selfish, huh?

Sadly, some of our poor parenting skills can be traced back to selfish thinking in our own lives. Here again we are dealing with that old enemy—selfishness. Don't we hate how it creeps its ugly head into every area of our lives that we are trying so hard to fill with love?

Discipline

God is true love, and He loves us unconditionally and disciplines us out of that love. Yes, I said He disciplines us.

> For whom the LORD loveth he chasteneth, and scourgeth every son whom he receiveth. If ye endure chastening, God dealeth with you as with sons; for what son is he whom the father chasteneth not? But if ye be without chastisement, whereof all are partakers, then are ye bastards, and not sons. Furthermore we have had fathers of our flesh which corrected us, and we gave them reverence: shall we not much rather be in subjection unto the Father of spirits, and live? For they verily for a few days chastened us after their own pleasure; but he for our profit, that we might be partakers of his holiness. Now no chastening for the present seemeth to be joyous, but grievous: nevertheless afterward it yieldeth the peaceable fruit of righteousness unto them which are exercised thereby.
>
> Hebrews 12:6-11

> Chasten thy son while there is hope, and let not thy soul spare for his crying.
>
> Proverbs 19:18

> He that spareth his rod hateth his son: but he that loveth him chasteneth him betimes.
>
> Proverbs 13:24

"Chasten" means "discipline." Please notice it says to discipline while there is hope because when children are young, they are pliable. Jean Burr, Ph.D., of Colby College and Rob Grunewald of the Federal Reserve Bank of Minneapolis reviewed and studied early childhood development and reported in 2006 that the quality of life an adult enjoys and even the contribution he or she makes to society can be traced back to his or her first few years of life. I find overwhelming evidence that a child is already programmed to how he or she is going to act the rest of his or her life by the time the child is four to five years old. While it is not an impossible task to "rehabilitate" an out-of-control child, it is much more preferable to bend the child in the right direction while he or she is still young and not set in his or her ways.

When our son Mathew was a toddler, he was an active young man who loved the word "no" because he took it as a challenge. One day Mathew had done something that I thought deserved the death penalty. I began to yell and scream and look for my spoon to make sure he would never again make the same mistake. (This was a few years before I began to be more pliable myself and discipline out of love and not anger.) I was zoning in on him, ready to mete out the most severe of spankings, when I heard the Lord speak to my heart and say, "He's mine. Bend him, Linda, don't break him."

I knew then that I needed to calm down and get myself under control. He was God's child. God had a purpose for Mathew, and if I was not careful, I could get in God's way by not disciplining him in the correct manner. Talk about being humbled.

As parents, we must never discipline out of anger, vowing to teach them a lesson. Yes, we need to teach them, but our lessons need to be taught out of the loving, pure motive of seeking their well-being, not out of our own need for justice.

Would we let our child play in the middle of the street? Why not? Because we love our child and want to protect him or her, right? The same is true for discipline.

The English Standard Version says it like this:

> ...He who loves him is diligent to discipline him.
>
> Proverbs 13:24

I love the word "diligent." To me, "diligent" means "to act quickly and with excellence." A diligent person is one who does things correctly and doesn't put it off. The same should be true with disciplining a child—don't put it off. Correction should be done immediately to make sure that the offense is connected with the punishment. Since God is our role model in all that we do, it is only natural that we pay close attention when He talks about the subject of discipline and learn from Him. How does God discipline? Always, and only in love and with great mercy and grace. He disciplines us for our good, not to show how strong He is.

As our sons grew older, the discipline grew more creative because when the boys did something that needed creative discipline, I would tell them to go to their rooms while I went to the Lord in my room.

I would get alone with God and say, "Here is what they did. What kind of discipline should I use?"

I knew that if I asked for wisdom according to James 1:5, God would give it to me liberally. I would get quiet and wait for an inner voice, an answer to my question, a solution for the problem from the Word Himself. Sometimes I would laugh at the methods of discipline that the Lord would come up with. I don't know why I was surprised—after all, He is the Creator of the universe!

When one of our sons was about twelve years old, he did something quite grievous. As parents, it called us to attention, to keep a close eye on his behavior and let him know that sin was not a game. I went into my room to pray, unsure of what the proper consequences should be for such a grievous offense. Shortly afterward, I came out and asked my husband to take my son's bedroom door off the hinges. As Dennis got his toolbox, our son cried out, "No, no, don't take off my door!" We didn't stop because he cried. We continued taking off the door, all the while explaining that when he started making wise choices and we'd seen a repentant heart, we would put the door to his room back on. But because we could not trust him, we had to leave the door off. What a difference that made in his life. The consequences seemed mild to us, but to him, it was a fate worse than death! It worked. The sin was never repeated, and we had peace in our home once again.

As you can see, our boys were not perfect. We really shouldn't expect perfection, but in cases of rebellion, we must be ready to discipline. Swift and correct discipline will bring peace to our home every time.

Isn't that what we all want, peace?

> Correct thy son, and he shall give thee rest; yea, he shall give delight unto thy soul.
>
> Proverbs 29:17

The New Living Translation says, ". . . they will give you peace of mind and will make your heart glad." Parents don't want to discipline, fearing the reactions from their children, friends, family, or even coworkers. Unfortunately, these are the same parents who never have peace in their home. When it comes to our children, we must always seek godly counsel. The world's way is certain death. We want abundant life for our children.

One of the biggest lies parents believe is that children hate discipline. This is just not true. Children love boundaries—it makes them feel safe, loved, and protected. The worst thing parents can do is be too lenient in the correction of their children. When this happens, the child will seek to find boundaries just to know they are there. No matter how they must find them, they will persist with bad behavior until the parents say stop.

Before we get too far into discipline, we need to clarify what discipline is and what it is not. Discipline is not abuse. "Discipline" is defined as "training that corrects, molds, or perfects the mental faculties or moral character."* The goal of discipline is and always should be to train, mold to form moral character.

"Abuse," however, is defined as "the improper or excessive use or treatment."** The goal of abuse is cruel, malicious, and merciless.

---

* Merriam-Webster's online dictionary, www.merriam-webster.com
** Merriam-Webster's online dictionary, www.merriam-webster.com

Another term we use is "conditioning." People use conditioning all the time and never realize it. Conditioning is "a simple form of learning involving the formation, strengthening, or weakening of an association between a stimulus and a response."*

Anyone can see that there is a huge difference between proper discipline and abuse. Since every child is different, discipline is different for every child. The goal is to train and mold. Disciplining our child should be effective and simple so that the response to discipline will bring about a change in behavior. Thus, discipline becomes conditioning, *consistent* conditioning.

Consistent Conditioning

Let me give you a few examples of how consistent discipline (conditioning) works:

> **Example 1:** Millie is two years old, and she likes to put keys in the light socket. Now, we all know that putting keys in the light socket could cause Millie great harm, so the discipline here must be swift and grave—we are disciplining Millie to save her from certain harm. We take the keys away from Millie and heavily tap her first three fingers. She cries, waits for a few minutes, and again picks up the keys and heads for the light socket. She wants to see if you will be consistent.

---

* Merriam-Webster's online dictionary, www.merriam-webster.com

By being consistent in our discipline, we are conditioning her that there is a negative response to putting the keys in the light socket. If she continues to try to put the keys in the light socket, we will continue to heavily tap her first three fingers. IF we are consistent, THEN she will stop trying to put the keys in the light socket. She will not be willing to pay the price (her aching fingers) for the folly of the keys.

> **Example 2:** Mike is three years old. He doesn't get his way one morning, so he throws himself on the floor, kicking and screaming. Most parents will ignore this behavior, reasoning that if we ignore a behavior, it will go away.

Beloved, I say with all meekness and love—this strategy will never work. When we ignore a behavior, it will just progress to a worse behavior until we are forced to take action. That's the way it works, and it will never change.

What do we do? If Mike is having a tantrum, we tell him to get off the floor, explain that his behavior is unacceptable, and let him know exactly what we plan to do if he does not comply with our direction. At this point, we have several different options, depending on our own beliefs.

1. First, we can pat Mike on his behind (nowhere else). A couple of swift, firm pats will do it.

2.   We can use an isolation method. Isolation works like this: We put Mike on a chair where he will be seated until he stops acting out completely. We give him a few minutes to do the appropriate thing. The appropriate thing here is a heart change—that means a change in attitude, looks included. If he says it's all better and he still growls at us, then he hasn't had a heart change. If he says it's all better and he is still yelling at us, then he hasn't had a heart change. We all know what a heart change looks like. The person's countenance will change, and he or she will soften inside and out.

3.   Let's say Mike doesn't change his attitude. THEN we pick him up and place him in a chair for two minutes. If he is persistent and whines, cries, and tries to get off the chair, then we simply put him back on the chair until he sits still. Once we have gained control of the situation and the child gains control of his flesh, we let him get off the chair.

When he doesn't get his way again and has another tantrum, do not let a second pass. We must do the same thing we did previously—only this time, lengthen his stay in the chair. We continue to apply immediate discipline. IF we are consistent, THEN the tantrums will stop.

If our choice is to pat, then we must be consistent in that, too. Every temper tantrum gets two or three swift, firm pats on the behind, and nowhere else . . . ever. The child will usually choose to do what is right over the discomfort of a few firm pats. Remember that discomfort to a three-year-old is not the same as discomfort to an adult. Never do we have the right to abuse our child in any situation. Any method of discipline we use needs to be the right decision for our family and needs to be done consistently.

Example 3: Jimmy is five years old and refuses to pick up his toys. We ask him very nicely to pick up his toys, but he doesn't move. We very calmly say, "Jimmy, either you pick up your toys, or I will put them in a box, and you won't see them for a week." We give him a few (not more than five) minutes to comply. Jimmy just looks at us and continues to play. We *calmly* find a box, place all of the toys that are on the floor into the box and place them in a garage or closet. We go to the calendar and put one line through every day Jimmy will be without his toys. Let him see the consequences of his behavior. No matter how he cries or begs, we don't give back the toys.

Let's say that the next day, we go through the same situation. We must simply and calmly do the same thing we did the day before. Do this consistently every day until Jimmy picks up his toys. What if Jimmy refuses to pick up his toys until he has no more toys? Then he has no more toys by his own choice. IF we are consistent, THEN he will get the picture. The loss of his toys will be greater than the temporary pain of having to pick them up.

Example 4: Kari is eight. We must realize that if we have lacked consistency all of her eight years, we have a lot of catching up to do. It will take a lot of work, but our child's life and future is worth the time and trouble we must endure for the present time. Let's say that Kari takes forever picking out an outfit for school, making mom late for an appointment and Kari late for school. In short, Kari is making the family's mornings a nightmare.

Give Kari thirty minutes' notice before bed that she needs to have an outfit laid out and ready for school the next morning. Explain that if she doesn't comply, then you will be picking an outfit out for her, without her help. Let her know that if you have to pick one out for her, she will wear that outfit to school. If after twenty minutes, she still hasn't complied, remind her that she has only ten minutes to have her outfit laid out, or you will be picking her outfit out for her.

When thirty minutes has passed, do just what you have promised to do. *Calmly* go to her closet and pick out an outfit. No matter how she begs, don't give in, and don't ask her opinion on the outfit.

Calmly explain she had plenty of warning and because she ignored the warnings and chose instead to be disobedient, she made the choice for you. It was obvious by her attitude she was unwilling to choose her own outfit. Explain sweetly that it is a task you are ready and willing to do for her. Don't waver; be consistent and calm.

Our experiences in handling past situations will determine the reaction today. If she is used to her parents giving in, then she will wail, cry, throw herself down, scream, beg, plead, and so on. Under no circumstance do we give in to this kind of behavior.

Advise her immediately that if she comes out of her room the following morning in any other outfit, then you will be picking her outfits out for the next week. Let's say all goes well, and she goes to school in the outfit you picked out. The next night, give her the same thirty minutes with the same consequences. If we have been lax in our decisions, we might have to go through this scenario more than one time. If we are consistent, I guarantee that she soon will be compliant and soon will be picking out an outfit for parental approval before bed each night.

Beware! If we ever stop being consistent, she will go back to her old ways, and we will have the same nightmare on our hands. Then it is entirely our responsibility; we are the one to blame for not following through. Remember that a child's consistently bad behavior is a direct result of poor parenting skills.

> **Example 5:** Jena is sixteen, and she wants a cell phone. We agree, setting some stipulations, including that she cannot take it to school. In any and every situation, we must explain the consequences right up front. Everyone has the right to know the price of an item before he or she purchases it. Children need to know

what the terms and conditions are so they can make a choice. Sometimes they are willing to pay the price, thinking it is worth the risk.

We are the ones in charge. If we see that the price isn't high enough to deter the behavior, we might need to up the price. If we are going to up the price, we must give notice ahead of time so that the child will know what the consequences will be. Remember, if we are consistent with making them pay the price, they will soon follow the rules instead of opting to try us at every turn.

The first week Jena has the phone, she takes it to school. We have already given her the rules and the consequences. The consequence for taking it to school was that she loses the phone for one week. Because Jena is not used to rules or our following through with our punishments, she might become belligerent and abusive. Don't give in now! We have trained her to bully us, and now we must face the bully we have made.

We calmly say, "If you continue to speak to me in that tone (or with that attitude), for every word you say, I will keep the phone an extra day." If she tries us, we must be consistent and firm.

If her behavior warrants her not having the phone for a month, then she goes without it for a month. It is ultimately her choice. Remember, we have set the price, and she knew the price before she broke the rules. One of two things is true—either she is ready and willing to pay the price we have set forth, or she doesn't think we will make her pay the price. Whichever is the case, the consequences do not change. We are not open to negotiation. We love her enough to be consistent and unyielding for her sake.

Before I go on, I feel we need to stop and be reminded that oftentimes, we parent the way we were parented. It is safe to say that many times, our example was not the best one. My parents disciplined with belts and switches. My mother was a screamer and loved to backhand us. We learned in the last chapter that we are taught how to be married from our parents. The same goes for parenting. One only has to have a glimpse of how I was raised to know how my boys suffered as very small children. We changed as we grew in the Word and found good parental role models to follow.

Please know that my parents did the best they could; they had only their parents' pattern to follow, so they were flawed from the beginning. Their CD of parenting was playing all that they had grown up with, so that is all they knew.

As in our marriages, many times, we know we don't want to parent the way we were parented, but we don't know how to make the necessary changes. How many times did we say when we were younger, "I will never do that (whatever that might be in our childhood) to my children." But sadly, we do the exact same thing to our own children that confused and frustrated us as children. We just don't know any better. We must break that cycle in our own children. But how do we do what we have never seen demonstrated?

Beloved, look to the Father. He never disciplines us for *His* good. He disciplines us for *our* good. He never disciplines us from anger, only love. He always lets us know the consequences of our behavior in advance so we know what price we will pay for our transgressions. He does not reject us when we make a mistake. God doesn't hold grudges against His children. He teaches us the importance of forgiveness. True repentance is something our children must be taught at a young age. Oh, the joy of a truly repentant child! Talk about peace in our homes!

Most importantly, Beloved, God is always consistent with us.

We don't have to parent the way we were parented. That is why I am writing this book. We can succeed at parenting by reading the Word, getting wise counsel, reading God-inspired books, and praying over our discipline choices. And don't forget to love unconditionally. Love never fails.

> **Example 6:** We had a really good example that just happened with our grandson, Micah, who is two years old. Micah's mom has been potty training Micah. One day he just decided he was not going to go to the potty. His mother tried everything she could think of, and yet, he was not detoured. Obviously, the price wasn't high enough.

Micah's mom was totally frustrated and ready to give up. I prayed quickly (as we are to do with all matters that need wisdom). Micah loved this four-by-four truck that he called his vroom-vroom. He played with it at our home every time he came over. I simply looked him in the eyes and told him if he kept peeing in his pants, I would put the vroom-vroom away. I asked him if he understood, and he said, "Yes." Although he is young, he knows that we are consistent in what we say and do with him.

The next day, when his mom put his underpants on him, he looked at her and said, "No potty in pants or vroom-vroom put away."

He didn't have one accident all day long! As a result of his great achievement, my husband picked him up after work and brought him to our house to ride his vroom-vroom. Good behavior should always be rewarded, especially when it is quick.

When teaching children's church years ago, I developed a saying that we have made a motto for children everywhere we teach: "Disobedience will always have consequences, but obedience always brings rewards."

I can hear someone now saying, "Rewarding is just bribery, and I shouldn't have to bribe my child to get him to do what is right."

Let's look first at the difference between bribery and reward. A bribe is "money or favor given or promised in order to influence the judgment or conduct of a person in a position of trust." In other words, you pay or promise someone so that you can unfairly get things to come out in your favor.

A reward is "a stimulus administered to an organism following a correct or desired response that increases the probability of occurrence of the response."

Rewarding sounds a lot like consistent conditioning, doesn't it? A bribe is to our advantage all of the time. However, a reward is neither solicited nor demanded. It is freely given to say, "What you did was fabulous! Please feel free to do it again!"

Consistent conditioning is so much more than just good discipline. A good teacher knows the value of true and heartfelt praise; children respond to praise that is sincere. When our child does something like picking up his toys before bedtime, and we didn't have to ask him to do it, we reward him with praise. For little ones, a loud and heartfelt praise like clapping and telling them how fabulous they really are can impact them so much. When we do this, we are sending a positive, consistent message—pick up your toys, and you will be rewarded. We must never let even the littlest of acts escape us. A polite, "Excuse me," a kind gesture, or a quick response to our instructions are all worthy of praise. We don't just discipline; we train. We are our children's first teacher. We don't just tell them to pick up their toys; we show them how. If they forget a toy, we are not angry. We are their teacher. We must show them how to check their rooms and ensure they have all their toys put away. We help them understand why we pick up our toys, because we love a safe and clean house, and picking up our toys is the way we get it done.

Having said that, we must also know that we love our children for who they are, not what they do. They must know that first and foremost. We show them love, no matter what. Yes, we will discipline, but we will discipline them in love. While we are trying to teach them to be successful children and grow into successful adults, we love them unconditionally.

When my sons shared with each other spontaneously, you would have thought they had just been named president of the United States of America! We almost had a parade! They were rewarded with loud and thunderous praise and sometimes even a small token of our appreciation for their effort and our joy.

Consequently, my sons are the most generous young men I know. They are not selfish, nor are they envious. They were trained to be happy when someone else prospered, to rejoice when someone else was blessed.

They didn't care about the reward, be it praise or a small toy. It was significant to them that they were being recognized for a job well done, and who among us doesn't love to be recognized for a job well done? Just because our children are children doesn't mean they are not people. Every one, regardless of age, needs to know he or she is appreciated and loved. If we are consistent in all that we do for our children, we will open wide the door to peace and happiness in our family.

Children know when we are not being consistent, even when we don't notice ourselves. We praise them for something on Sunday and don't even notice the same act on Monday. We discipline our child for hitting his brother on Monday and let it go on Tuesday.

Incoherent parenting will lead to confused, frustrated, and rebellious children. Children who do not know exactly what is expected of them are going to be in a constant state of confusion and frustration. Soon this confusion and frustration will lead to apathy and rebellion.

Children truly don't understand consequences or rewards when they are disciplined for something one day, and the next day, the same thing passes as good behavior. Not understanding what is expected of them, children soon become indifferent to our instructions. This apathy will be followed by rebellion, defiance against our authority as parents, an authority they do not trust to be wise or prudent.

One of the definitions for "prudent" is "**carefully considering consequences:** using good judgment to consider likely consequences and acting accordingly." Wow! A parent who uses wisdom with consistency is a child's dream parent. We will learn more about that trust in the next chapter. Beloved, it is clear that when we aren't consistent with discipline and reward our children, then the children cannot be held responsible for their behavior.

As a parent, we have to be vigilant and consistent in everything we do. Now we know why there are so few success stories when it comes to raising children—because it takes diligent effort on the parent's part. Good parenting requires hard work and consistency.

Sadly, we are a microwave society. We want things right now. A drive-through mentality will not work in raising successful, obedient, happy, and well-adjusted children.

Envision, if you will, Thanksgiving dinner. This fabulous, once-a-year meal is meticulously planned for weeks. We want the right menu, the right china, and the right appetizers, and we wouldn't dare skimp on the desserts! A smart cook will usually make extra dessert and hide it away for another day—or is that just me? Beloved, planning an extravagant meal like this is not for amateurs or the faint of heart.

We plan, shop, plan some more, then we start a week in advance expertly crafting each dish. This meal will be talked about for weeks. We cannot miss a detail. Thanksgiving Day is not a meal just for that day. Yes, it is to be abundantly savored and slowly enjoyed all day Thursday. But we also look forward to eating those delectable leftovers for days to come. One year, the leftovers were gone early Friday morning, and there was almost a riot in our home!

We work diligently for weeks for that one day, but then, if planned right, we don't have to cook for a week afterward. Ah! The sweet rest that good Thanksgiving leftovers bring!

If we prepare our children well for life, they will be like a good Thanksgiving meal. Yes, it takes a lot of time and planning. We have to be well-prepared; we don't want to be caught without a crucial ingredient when the recipe calls for it. But a good cook plans ahead. So does a good parent.

Some people give more thought to their Thanksgiving meals than they do their children's lives. We know what a great pleasure it is when people notice the effort we put into planning that one Thanksgiving meal. Those compliments are our greatest reward. The same applies to our children. If planned correctly, they will be like the Thanksgiving leftovers; they will give you sweet rest after years of hard work.

Yes, the younger years are hard, long days of planning and preparing, but with consistency comes rest. When the children start to grow older, they will know we have our priorities right and we will always do our best to be consistent.

Much like we respect the person who can pull off that perfect Thanksgiving meal, our children will respect a parent who is on their side every day of their lives and is not willing to take the easy way out.

Anyone can make instant mashed potatoes, but a faithful cook will take the time to make the real thing. And everyone knows the difference. Children are the same way. They know when we care enough to be consistent, taking the time to raise them with great prudence. They might not tell us while they are young, but they will look back and appreciate and respect us for taking the time to make that consistent investment in their lives. That investment made today will generate a huge dividend in the future.

What a joy our sons and our daughters-in-law are to us! They are constantly a blessing, and we have such peace and happiness in our family. Every time we get together, the love and joy is so magnified that we don't know how it can get any better—and then it does.

Thank God we listened and obeyed years before. We worked diligently when our children were young, and now we see the fruit of our labor. Godly children and godly grandchildren are in themselves a great reward. Our prayer is that our grandchildren will be so obedient to their parents that it will be second nature to them to be obedient to their Father in heaven.

While we love those compliments we hear at Thanksgiving, it is more desired to hear the Father say, "Well done, My good and faithful servant. Enter into the joy of the Lord."

The Third Pillar

The Pillar of Demonstration

The aged women likewise, that they be in behaviour as becometh holiness, not false accusers, not given to much wine, teachers of good things; that they may teach the young women to be sober, to love their husbands, to love their children, to be discreet, chaste, keepers at home, good, obedient to their own husbands, that the word of God be not blasphemed.

Titus 2:3-5

This is a true saying, if a man desire the office of a bishop, he desireth a good work. A bishop then must be blameless, the husband of one wife, vigilant, sober, of good behaviour, given to hospitality, apt to teach; Not given to wine, no striker, not greedy of filthy lucre; but patient, not a brawler, not covetous; One that ruleth well his own house, having his children in subjection with all gravity; (For if a man know not how to rule his own house, how shall he take care of the church of God?) Not a novice, lest being lifted up with pride he fall into the condemnation of the devil. Moreover he must have a good report of them which are without; lest he fall into reproach and the snare of the devil. Likewise must the deacons be grave, not doubletongued, not given to much wine, not greedy of filthy lucre; Holding the mystery of the faith in a pure conscience. And let these also first be proved; then let them use the office of a deacon, being found blameless. Even so must their wives be grave, not slanderers, sober, faithful in all things. Let the deacons be the husbands of one wife, ruling their children and their own houses well.

1 Timothy 3:1-12

A FTER YEARS OF TEACHING children, we have found that when we use visuals, the child can and will almost always remember the story and recall important details. That is why in a really good children's curriculum, there is always an object lesson or a visual to get the child's attention and help him/her retain the information. Being a parent is like being a constant visual. We are a live movie being shown every minute of the day to our children. What we do is a live demonstration for our children to learn by and repeat in their own lives.

Today more than ever, people make choices because they are convenient—not because they are right. We are a microwave mentality society. Too often we want to take the easiest route in everything we do. The easiest way is not necessarily the right way.

As parents, we don't have the luxury of always doing what is convenient. Sometimes doing what is convenient means making a compromise, and although we are taught to make compromises in our everyday lives, compromising when it comes to our children and the lives we lead in front of them can cause great confusion to a watchful child. And children are always watching.

When our children were young and able to answer the phone, Dennis told them one evening to tell someone that he wasn't home. Our child was obedient and lied. As soon as our son put down the receiver, Dennis and I had a heated discussion over what had just transpired in our home. I said that he had just taught our son to lie. Dennis, however, felt it was an acceptable lie, one he had heard and seen adults tell children to do many times in his youth. Remember our previous chapter on our CD—Dennis's CD had many instances of this happening, and in none of them was this kind of thing frowned on or thought of as unacceptable. We came to an agreement and used that incident to instruct the boys that it was never right to lie. The next time someone called and one of the boys answered, Dennis told them to say he was not available for the caller. This was the truth; he was busy with his family and not available for that caller. Peace reigned once more.

What we do speaks louder than what we say. Our children are watching us more than they are listening to us. How many times have we heard wise men say that actions speak louder than words? What are our actions saying to our children? Let's stop and examine ourselves. Have we ever lied to people in front of our children, then made excuses for it? When we make excuses for sin, we are trying to cover it up. The only way to be truly free is to uncover sin, acknowledge it, and repent.

I was watching one of those hidden camera shows recently, and there, in the ever-seeing eye of the camera, was a man using his young daughter to rob a store. This poor child was no more than five years old and was already a thief. The father had taken this sweet young preschooler and turned her into a criminal. He was showing her how to be untrustworthy, an outcast in society, and a corrupt adolescent before she was even in school! While this is an unusual situation, it really shows the power of demonstration as a parent. We all need to be agonizingly aware of what we are teaching our children through our own actions.

Some weeks ago, I watched as a young mother was shopping in our local grocery store. As she was walking through the store, she was feeding her child grapes that she had not yet purchased. It ought to be painfully obvious to anyone with any modicum of sense that when she gets to the register and the grapes are weighed, it will be short quite a few ounces. Beloved, this is called stealing. This mother was quietly, perhaps unknowingly, teaching her daughter to steal from the store and not giving it a second thought.

It bothers me greatly to see parents walking through the store, feeding their children from boxes and bags of not yet purchased food because of the demonstration pillar they are forming. There is a deeper problem here than just eating from a not-yet-paid-for box or eating a few grapes. When parents choose to demonstrate this kind of behavior, they are reinforcing the belief in their children that they don't have to wait for anything. Everything is theirs for the taking, no matter who it belongs to. They can have whatever they want, whenever they want, regardless of the laws of the land or the authority over that land.

We are giving our children a sense of entitlement that will follow them for the rest of their lives. And then we wonder why they are so impatient and demanding. We made them that way.

That store this woman was in belonged to someone. It does not matter if that business makes a zillion dollars a day; we have no right to take advantage of that business owner.

Parents say they teach their children not to steal, and then turn around and say things like, "This store makes a million dollars a day. They won't miss this one thing." What if everyone had that attitude? Our prices would skyrocket, and our stores would close.

When I worked at a donut store as a teenager, I sadly didn't understand this principle. Well, maybe I did, but I didn't think it was very important. This donut store made the best donuts I had ever tasted. The rule of the store was when you closed, you could take home whatever donuts were left. Unfortunately, for me, my favorite donuts were everyone else's favorite donuts. So when I saw that my favorite donuts were getting low, I would box up some and set them aside. One day the owner, a wonderful woman, asked me what they were for. I told her that they were for a later customer. That was a lie! They were for me! I had reckoned within myself that the rule was I could have whatever was left, and since I was the last customer in the store and they were left, I could take them home guilt-free. It wasn't long before I felt so guilty, I had to stop. I knew what I was doing was wrong, but I so loved those donuts. Remember in the last chapter, we talked about being drawn away by our own lusts? I really did lust for those donuts. We cannot sugarcoat sin. No matter how good it might taste going down, it is still sin.

After that, if I wanted a donut that I knew wasn't going to be there, I either set it back for my lunch (which was acceptable), or when that donut-loving customer picked it out, I waved good-bye to my donut friend and went on my way.

Thank God, I have grown in the Lord over the years. Before you judge my donut days too harshly, please read on.

A few years back, I shopped at our local Wal-Mart and made several purchases. It was my habit (and still is) that before I left the store, I would check my receipt and make sure the purchases rang up at the right price. That day, I was in a hurry and didn't check my receipt until I arrived at home. After checking my receipt, I noticed that I was not charged for a soccer ball that I had purchased.

I searched frantically on the receipt for the price of the ball. Money was tight, and I didn't want to have to pay out more than I should. But after checking the receipt ten times or more, there was no sign of the ball ever being rung up. I set the ball aside and told the boys they couldn't open the ball until I could take it back to the store and pay for it.

A few days later, I took the ball and the receipt of my purchases from that day back to Wal-Mart and went to the customer service department. I told them what had happened, showed them my receipt, and asked them to charge me for the ball. The girl behind the counter just stared at me in disbelief.

"You want to exchange the ball?" she said.

"No. You didn't charge me for it; I want to pay for it," I explained for the fourth time.

"You want us to charge you for the ball—really?" she couldn't believe it.

"I have children at home that need to be taught honesty," I explained.

She complied blankly, not really understanding what had just happened. But I walked out of that Wal-Mart a tall woman, a woman who had integrity, a mother who cared more about her children than the price of a soccer ball. This lesson was invaluable to my children, and the lady in Wal-Mart never forgot me. I could have accidentally walked out of that store with a thousand-dollar item in my pocket, and she would have not called the police. My children and the store clerk all learned a strong lesson in the pillar of demonstration. It was a win-win situation.

Good character and a good name are worth more money than anyone can make in their lifetime. We might want to ask ourselves what kind of character we demonstrate. Our children know. They have been watching us all of their lives. Where do we think they learned the things that they do? They didn't just come up with their speech or their actions out of thin air. Someone somewhere demonstrated these things to them. If we want to know how we act, we need only look as far as our children. They are a mirror of us, a small version of who we really are when no one is looking.

When a parent complains about his or her child's behavior, the parent must only look as far as his or her home. There are many things in our home that shape our children's conduct. Find any preschooler, and start singing a song that child hears on his or her favorite morning show, and the child will sing along word for word. While most of these songs are harmless, the bigger picture here is that we have let television shape our children's moral fiber.

One of the leading opportunities we find for offensive in our home is our television set. What do we watch in front of our children? Do we watch men and women whose only ambitions are to bed anyone and everyone they can? It's problematic to teach children that fornication is wrong when we find it so funny on the sitcoms every evening. Sexual perversions of every nature are being used as gag lines on nearly every sitcom and prime time movie. Even our commercials are rampant with nudity and suggestive sexual behavior. Mom and Dad, we need to screen what our children are watching day and night.

We can hardly watch a TV show today without hearing unbridled profanity, yet we are teaching our children that profanity is wrong. Right? Once that language has found a place in our home, it will find a place in our child's vocabulary. See the dilemma?

> A double minded man is unstable in all his ways.
>
> James 1:8a

We must set our standards firmly and resist seesawing back and forth in our thinking and actions, or we won't be established in any area of our lives. There will be no part of our lives where we have peace—none. Dear ones, this is a dangerous situation. A home without peace is not a place to raise victorious children.

Many years ago, they used to have all the risqué shows on late at night when the children were supposed to be in bed. Now, these R-rated shows are on all hours every day of the week—100 channels of filth twenty-four seven.

When we were raising our sons, we made a decision early on that they would never have a TV in their room. Our family TV was in the living room, where everyone could see what was on and where we, as parents, could monitor the content, if needed. Now so many children, even preschoolers, have a TV in their rooms and have the ability to watch whatever they please, whenever they please…without any adult supervision.

Beloved, this is like inviting the devil to babysit our children. While we know we would never do that, we turn on our TV and turn off our common sense, not giving a thought to what we are entertaining in our own homes.

I cannot count the television shows that were off-limits in our home when our children were young. Even now, when we have no children in our home, there are still countless shows that are off-limits because of their sexual content or language.

When thinking of demonstration, something we usually never think about is political satire. When it comes to political satire and the president of the United States, how many of us have heard and seen open ridicule and disdain aimed viciously at our leaders? But as believers, we teach our children, according to 1 Timothy 2:1-3, to pray for those who are in authority. We can't pray for our leaders and mock them at the same time. That would make us double-minded. We don't have to agree with everything our governmental leaders do, but it is mandated in the Word that we pray for them, an action that God assures us will bring us peace.

Our family is passionate about our dearly loved America. All of our children (daughters included) are zealous about this country and its people and would make the most excellent politicians. History and government are some of our favorite dinnertime discussions. If there is an issue that I need more information on, I simply call one of them, and I can be sure to have the needed answers from every conceivable point of view in no time. And while there are issues on which we disagree with each other, we all stand strong in our love for our country. The young people in our home will hear conversations that downgrade or treasure our country, our beliefs, and our nation's great history and Christian heritage.

We had a president some years back that lacked self-control and integrity. While I didn't vote for him, it was my duty to give him the respect that his office was due. Hearing this taught my children volumes when it came to respecting authority. It wasn't always easy. But remember—saying and doing what is right are not always the easiest things to do, but they are always the right things to do.

People don't know the seriousness of demonstrating respect of authority to their children. An actress who was on a daytime talk show delighted in blatantly and loudly mocking the president of the United States. She boasted that in her home, he was called all sorts of derogatory names. She openly bragged about the teacher's concern over her young son's language when it came to the president. She told her son's teacher that he didn't have to respect the office of the president and was encouraged to use insulting remarks about the president.

Beloved, we live in the United States of America, where we have the privilege of disagreeing with our leaders and their policies. We can do it openly and at whatever volume we choose. That is what makes this country so magnificent. But we are not talking about freedom of speech in this chapter; we are talking about how we, as parents, shape our children through our lives and our actions.

This actress was openly satisfied that she was demonstrating to her children their power to defy and dishonor authority. My friend, this is beyond dangerous. This poor confused woman has no clue that she is the authority in her home and, while she is demonstrating to them how to dishonor authority, she is teaching them to dishonor her and all authority.

When children have no respect for authority, they also have no boundaries for decent and ethical behavior. In other words, they are unaffected by rules and consequences. They don't have to listen to anyone, even their mommy, in this case, because their mommy told them so!

It doesn't matter who the authority is, if someone has legal authority in our society—teachers, pastors, store managers, police officers, or crossing guards—and they are not asking us to sin, then we need to respect the authority of that person's office.

We've all heard of children who openly mock the police, their teachers, and their bus driver, showing respect for no one. This happens because they have learned to be disrespectful by someone's example. We wonder why our youths have no respect for their elders. They are only doing what they have been taught.

About ten years ago, I was working in the administrative office at a local public school when a kindergartener was brought into the office by a teacher's aide. The child was aggressive, loud, and unruly. He had kicked and cursed his teacher and the teacher's aide—the latter of which had the hazardous job of bringing the child to the office. When she brought him into the office, he attempted to do the same thing to the office staff. This was his second trip to the office that day. He had been counseled by the assistant principal, given a verbal reprimand, and sent back to class. An hour later, he was back in the office exhibiting the same shocking behavior, and the only choice was to suspend this child.

His parents were called and asked to come and pick him up, but they were too busy. A grandmother was then called, and she was irate with the school that they would suspend this child for "such a small infraction." She thought he should be given another chance and sent back to class. She, too, rebuffed the assistant principal and refused to stop what she was doing and come and get this young child.

Here was a child who had only been alive for five years, and yet he was belligerent, disrespectful, disobedient, full of anger, and already marked as a trouble maker. How did he get this way? Neither his parents nor his grandparents could be bothered by him or his problems. None of the adults in his family had shown any respect for the rules and regulations of the school, knowing they were supposed to go and get him. They refused to do what they were asked.

The criminal here is not the child, but the adults who are in charge of the child. This child is only five—he didn't start out his life with such disrespect for authority. He was taught to be disrespectful. He didn't start out spewing curse words when he was a baby; he learned those words. What else have these parents and grandparents taught this five-year-old? What will this child's life be like when he is fifteen? Where will this angry young man be in ten years without proper teaching?

Without the proper influence and guidance, this wayward young man will most likely be in jail, another sad statistic of youth crime. He will be labeled a criminal, yet he is only doing what he was taught at home. The parents will shake their heads

95

and perhaps blame the school system, the community, or even the government. But the fault lies squarely with the parents and grandparents. This child is not the first generation to be belligerent; he is the third generation—the third generation disobedient, third generation disrespectful, and third generation defiant. Regrettably, given time and no teaching, there will most certainly be a fourth generation of the same.

As soon as our grandson Micah could recognize the police cars in our city, we told him that they were our friends and they were there to help us and we loved them. One day, an officer came to our home to do a safety inspection, and Micah was there.

He saw the officer, and I asked him, "Micah, what are the police?"

He quickly responded, "Friend."

The officer smiled, thinking how cute this two-year-old was. I smiled, too, but for a different reason. I knew this young child was learning to respect authority. That, my friend, is priceless.

At the young age of two, Micah was already being taught respect for law enforcement. As a teenager, he will have had years of demonstration concerning honoring and respecting authority. Our expectations and prayers are that he will have too much respect for the law, the officers, and the people who have authority over him to cross that line. The only way he can acquire this type of respect is if we teach it and demonstrate our respect and love for those who have authority over us.

The profession of teaching today is far different from what it was years ago. If you were a teacher in our community, you were held with the highest regard by students and parents alike. Teachers knew what was going on in every home in their classroom and had a great effect on those homes.

Teaching today is different in so many ways. Families are different. In the past, when a teacher said something, it was never questioned by the parents. Rules were rules, and a student needed to follow them. Parents stood behind the teachers, and the teachers stood behind the parents. It was, most times, a beautiful relationship that benefited the student for the rest of his life. The student was being taught respect for authority and didn't even realize it. The parents were teaching it and didn't even realize it. It was just right, and it worked. The schools' biggest problem back then was the gum chewing! How things have changed.

As a teacher, I heard a lot of creative excuses as to why homework did not get done, and I am sure it was the same way years ago. But now, the excuses come directly from the parents. I never had a chance to request assignments from some children because their parents were in my classroom before school even started, telling me why the assignment wasn't done. Sometimes I knew the parent wasn't being truthful. Many times, it was because the parents were out late and had the children with them. Subsequently, because everyone was tired after returning from a late night, the children were told by the parents that they didn't have to do their homework. All too frequently, the family had such a hectic lifestyle that they just didn't take the time to do the homework. It's not as important to understand why the family was always busy; it's more important to look at the outcome. When a parent told his or her child that the child didn't need to do something the teacher (an authority) told him or her to do, the parent was demonstrating a lack of respect for authority. Here again, let us not lose focus. We are not talking about the amount of homework kids have today or the quality of teachers we have today. We are talking about teaching our children to respect authority so they can live in peace. If parents display a lack of respect for authority, the children will naturally do the same.

Making excuses for our children can be a dangerous habit to get started. Here again, we are demonstrating something that could be detrimental to them later in life. Once we had a family visit our home, and they had a four-year-old son who was into everything. This young man wasn't just a busy child; he was destructive. His parents kept making excuses for his behavior: He was excited to be in our home, he was tired, he had just played with his neighbor, and that always worked him up. . . . He was an uncontrollable little boy with no boundaries, and excuses were all these poor parents had to give.

Parents don't realize that often, when we make excuses for our children, we are really making excuses for ourselves and for our woefully absent parenting skills. While it is natural to try to explain away our child's wrong behavior or poor character, it does them more harm than good in the end because we are not correcting the behavior, just making excuses for it. How much better would our society be if instead of excusing a poor choice a child made, we helped them to make better choices. That cannot be done by making excuses for them. It can only be done by revealing the flawed behavior as incorrect, in love, and correcting it.

Kids instinctively know when they can get away with misbehaving, especially in public. Most children are extremely clever and have tested the waters enough to realize that their parents will think of the correct excuse for whatever or whoever it is they choose to challenge—thus making it all right. Beloved, again, making excuses for our children will not help them in the long run. We are only demonstrating to them how to make excuses for themselves.

Years ago in our community, this was literally the case when an elderly woman was murdered by a young teen. He killed the woman because she complained about his loud music as she was passing him on the sidewalk. He took offense at the fact that this eighty-something-year-old woman would dare say his music was too loud. He was angry, so he beat her to death, right there on the sidewalk. He savagely beat this poor woman's life right out of her, all because she said his music was too loud.

This young man displayed no respect for authority, no reverence for his elders, and no feeling or emotion toward human life. When his trial started, his lawyers came up with several things that they said excused his behavior. They blamed his music, alcohol, a pill he was taking, and anger issues. The attorneys revealed that this was not the young man's first run-in with the authorities in his life. This young man clearly had a problem with authority and boundaries. As in too many cases where the child has no respect for authority or clear boundaries, he soon finds those boundaries in the court system.

It also was revealed that this young man was diagnosed with oppositional defiant disorder, or ODD.

In 1980, the American Psychiatric Association (APA) created oppositional defiant disorder and defined it as "a pattern of negativistic, hostile and defiant behavior." The official symptoms of ODD include:

- Frequent temper tantrums
- Excessive arguing with adults
- Active defiance and refusal to comply with adult requests and rules
- Deliberate attempts to annoy or upset people
- Blaming others for his or her mistakes or misbehavior
- Often being touchy or easily annoyed by others
- Frequent anger and resentment
- Mean and hateful talking when upset
- Seeking revenge

Interestingly, one of the main treatments for ODD is parental training!

Let me park my bicycle here for one moment and say that these "symptoms" are normal childhood behavior. This is what we are attempting to tweak. We want our children to be able to express themselves, but not in anger or in a sinful manner. Children are children, and they need to be taught. We are the teachers. Children will try and test us; we must be prepared to meet that test with a firm and loving answer. When one test is over, we will be on to another test. Dear ones, this is called active parenting.

We might just look at that list and ask ourselves, "How many of those things did we do when we were children? After doing some of those things, were we corrected by our parents or someone in authority?"

Now, look at the list again. The things we did that weren't corrected, do we still do them? We know we don't have ODD, but what we might have is a pattern of behavior that needs correcting. In some circles, it would be called sin, and rightfully so.

How many of us are touchy and easily annoyed with others? The cure?

> Beloved, let us love one another: for love is of God; and every one that loveth is born of God, and knoweth God. He that loveth not knoweth not God; for God is love.
>
> 1 John 4:7-8

> Thou shalt love thy neighbour as thyself.
>
> Matthew 22:39b

A far cry from mental illness, huh? On a lighter note, I look at that list and think of my brothers. We would be in the car going on a road trip, or just around the corner, and one of us just couldn't keep our hands to ourselves. One of us would touch the other one just to get a reaction. Now it is hilarious to recall, but at the time, it was sheer torture—torture to be the one being touched, not torture to be the toucher! Of course, we stopped doing that behavior as children, solely because our mother made it inadvisable to continue. Smile!

By 1980, there were a large number of American parents who had not been taught how to parent. Teenagers were continuing to display symptoms of things that should have long been corrected as children. So to excuse the behavior, the APA came up with a label. Although parent training is the main treatment, drugging the child is considered acceptable treatment as well.

While I realize there are legitimate cases where a child is benefited from medication, this is a treatment that is used far too often in dealing with wayward children. Too many times, this is the easy way out for parents and teachers alike. Drugging our children is not teaching them. We are only postponing the inevitable, which is the fact that they must learn acceptable behavior in order to become a functioning healthy adult.

No matter the treatment, the parents now had an excuse for their children's behavior. It was not the parents' fault or their responsibility. There was something wrong with their child. Excusing wrong behavior and not requiring consequences for wrongdoing sets children up for a horrible fall later.

As I get back on my bicycle, we will continue our young man's story. This young man not only bludgeoned this elderly woman, he returned the next day to burn her body so he would leave no fingerprints. He then bragged to his friends about what he had done.

If parents look for and allow excuses for their children's wayward behavior, it is the parents who are responsible for the consequences. However, in the end, it is the children who pay the price. This young man's price was to spend the rest of his life in prison.

When we know we have done something wrong, we must acknowledge the wrong in order to be able to correct it. When our boys were young and did something wrong, the first thing they had to do was acknowledge what they had done, then apologize for the wrongdoing, then make amends. We tried hard never to make an excuse for their wrong behavior. Wrong behavior is just that—wrong. Wrong behavior should never be excused; it should be corrected. When wrong behavior is not corrected, it will continue to escalate out of control.

If we are making excuses for our children, we must quit immediately. We must take responsibility and change how we approach that wrong behavior. We need to acknowledge it to fix it. This will only work in our child's life if we are willing to demonstrate this concept in our own lives. We, as parents, must quit making excuses for our own bad behavior. We show our children how to acknowledge wrong decisions and bad behavior by demonstrating it ourselves.

Teaching our children to do the right thing in the right way with the right attitude is giving them the tools to change their life decisions and thereby change their destiny. This is where the rubber meets the road. Demonstration means everything, and that is where our children will learn the greatest life lessons.

Let us look at our own lives. When we make a wrong choice, do we acknowledge it to our family, or do we get defensive and dare anyone to say a word? Are we willing to humble ourselves in front of our family, our friends, or even strangers? Many of us are not willing to apologize for anything. Parents who will never grow or change usually don't think they need to change because, in their minds, they have done nothing wrong.

I'm sure we are all saddened at watching the behavior of children who have learned to be stubborn, prideful, and unapologetic. The best remedy is for each of us, as parents, to admit to our own mistakes and change that song on our child's CD. As we demonstrate humility in admitting our mistakes and wrong actions, we turn off that song that keeps rehearsing in our child's soul that says, "Don't take responsibility for anything. Never show remorse. You are right no matter what."

What is to happen to the poor child who has that song playing and doesn't know how to stop it?

At one point in my life, it became apparent to me that I had a problem in this area. It was difficult, but I made the decision to change. I vowed that when I did something wrong or made a bad decision, I would acknowledge it and, if needed, ask forgiveness. It wasn't easy in the beginning, but with time and wisdom, it became easier.

By opening yet another prison door of my childhood and changing my own CD, I set free future generations and changed their CD in the process. It can be done! As parents, when we win a battle over a fault or sin, we gain the factory for ourselves and for every generation that follows after us.

Beloved, we cannot demonstrate the right thing if we don't know how. If we see we have a weakness when it comes to demonstrating godly character to our children, we should not be ashamed to seek help. We can be sharpened by our time absorbing the Word, and change is especially forthcoming when we pray and ask God to show us where we need to fix a few areas in our own lives. Every one of us, as a parent, has room for improvement. Look around—is there someone in our church or our temple that is more mature than we are and has wisdom in this area? Why not spend some time with that person? We will never achieve perfection, but we need to keep tweaking ourselves in order to better teach our own children.

We have to be that good example for our children. Even though it is inconvenient and hard work, we need to fight to always do the right thing. Our children will still have to go through tests and trials in this life, but their battles will be fewer and shorter and their victories more extraordinary because we took the time to demonstrate how to live a decent, honest, and genuine life in front of them—not just for our success and peace, but for theirs also.

The Fourth Pillar

The Pillar of Trust

The just man walketh in his integrity: his children are blessed after him.

Proverbs 20:7

Better is the poor that walketh in his integrity, than he that is perverse in his lips, and is a fool.

Proverbs 19:1

Our fathers trusted in thee: they trusted, and thou didst deliver them.

Psalm 22:4

LORD, who shall abide in thy tabernacle? who shall dwell in thy holy hill?

He that walketh uprightly, and worketh righteousness, and speaketh the truth in his heart.

Psalm 15:1-2

For thou art my hope, O LORD GOD: thou art my trust from my youth.

Psalm 71:5

And again, I will put my trust in him. And again, Behold I and the children which God hath given me.

Hebrews 2:13

Deliver my soul, O LORD, from lying lips, and from a deceitful tongue.

Psalm 120:2

TRUST IS AN IMPORTANT key to opening the door to successful relationships.

Trust is the key to every relationship in heaven and on Earth. The parent/child relationship is no different. If a child does not trust his or her parent, that child will not obey. If the child will not obey his or her parents or any authority because of trust issues, the child will never be successful.

It is impossible to pick and choose which pillars we are going to use when it comes to parenting our children—it is all or nothing at all. However, we can choose which one we need to work on and adjust the most, and focus on that for a while so that we are able to become a better parent in that particular area.

Think of the people you trusted with your deepest, darkest secret when you were young. Were your parents in that group of people? In most cases, the answer is no. When children get into trouble, usually they go directly to their friends. Why? Their friends are the same age with the same wisdom and life experiences, and yet they will go to them for advice over a parent every time.

When a child is in crisis, he or she needs someone with a different view, someone with a multiplicity of life experiences from which to draw. The child needs someone who has been there and done that, yet children ignore the adult population altogether and go to the source they trust. Their peers are not necessarily the right source, but they usually trust their friends the most.

Kids will tell you that the reason they don't go to their parents when they need advice or they are in trouble is because they are afraid. There are three different kinds of fear a child might encounter when talking about the pillar of trust.

The first is a very real fear that stems from a pattern of irrational behavior demonstrated by their parents in the past. When faced with problems in their children's lives or in their own lives, the parents become irrational. In plain words, a child may have a parent who usually responds to the child by going off the deep end, yelling, screaming, flailing, cursing, or even becoming violent. In this case, a child's fear is reasonable. The parent consistently demonstrated that he or she cannot be trusted to be calm and rational, so the child is afraid to go to the parent under any circumstance.

The second kind of fear when it comes to the pillar of trust is when the child may not fear that his or her parent will be irrational, but the child also knows he or she cannot trust the parents to be wise. Perhaps in the past, the child went to the parent for advice or mentioned a problem, and the parent's response was half listening with a quick answer that had no foundation in wisdom whatsoever. In plain words, going to the parent for advice is a huge waste of the child's time. In this case, the fear is that the parent doesn't have enough experience himself or herself to give wise counsel or will not take the time to truly listen and try to understand the real problem. The child feels he or she is better off with friends' advice. The child reasons that at least his or her friends know what is going on in the child's world and takes the friends seriously when they talk.

Beloved, when our children come to us, we should be humbled and privileged that they would trust us enough to share. Knowing that we have the awesome responsibility to mold their very lives should give us great pause. These kids don't want a friend to help them; they want a parent to guide them. There is a difference, and we need to be aware of that difference.

The third kind of fear the child might be feeling is the fear that the parent cannot or will not keep the trust of the child. The child comes to a parent with a problem or concern, and the parent listens. The parent doesn't go off the deep end, and he or she has some real advice. Then, in the most public of situations, the child hears the parent talking to someone and retelling the same information the child shared with the parent in confidence. In simple words, the parent cannot be trusted with any information because the parent cannot keep his or her mouth shut. In this case, the child is afraid of having his or her most intimate and personal information told around the water cooler, at the dinner table, or in a random phone call.

In each of these situations, the basis of the child's fear really has to do with the pillar of trust. The only way a child will completely trust a parent is to experience repeatedly that the parent will consistently be there no matter what or no matter when. In every instance, the parent will listen, be a source of true wisdom, and know how to keep the child's confidence.

Most children's problems are benign and juvenile. But to a child, they are daunting, unsurpassable mountains because of the child's lack of wisdom and life experience. When a child is sharing a matter, he or she really needs to know we are listening and that we take them seriously.

> **Example #1:** Your daughter Julie comes to you and says that her best friend wears makeup to school and her mother doesn't know it. This is your chance to teach Julie about lying and about obedience and its rewards. You don't need to go to her friend's parents and spill your guts. Let them raise their daughter, and you raise yours. Julie obviously knew what her friend was doing wrong, and who knows, perhaps this is just the tip of

the iceberg with her friend. Keep your cool, and you will soon know everything. But first, Julie needs to know she can trust you with the little things. Keep these things in the back of your mind. Julie's friend has shown herself to be deceptive and rebellious. Don't overreact; just take note. You might need to recall this information later. But for now, be cool, listen, and use Julie's friend as a teaching tool for Julie.

Example #2: Your son, Kevin, comes to you and says that there is a group of boys smoking on his bus. After listening to every word he says, you ask him if smoking is allowed on the bus. Of course, you know the answer is no. You might talk about the danger of smoking on the bus and say that young children could get hurt. Encourage him to do the right thing on his own. Work on a plan together of whom he might tell anonymously and how to go about doing it. Let him know that if he can't turn these kids in, you can. Promise that you will be discreet, but this kind of thing must be addressed. Let him decide what to do and how to do it; empower him to be trustworthy himself.

Example #3: Your daughter, Samantha, tells you her friend's dad is abusing her. After a long heart-to-heart with Samantha about the laws, her friend's safety, and her responsibility as a friend, you and Samantha go straight to the authorities. In some cases, a trust might need to be broken for the greater good. A child comes to us because the child knows he or she can trust us to do the right thing. We are the parents, and we need to use wisdom. If a child comes to us with something that the authorities or another parent needs to know, we need to have the good judgment not to withhold information from the proper people. We are bound by the law of the land and our morals to make the hard decisions. This is our job as a parent—take the heat off of our child and make any and all decisions that our child doesn't have the maturity and wisdom to make because of his or her age and lack of life experience.

There was a young teenager who had severe trust issues with her mother. The mother asked her if there were any boys that she might like or have a crush on that she knew. The girl told her mother about a young man that she really liked. The mother went berserk! She began to yell at the girl, saying that she was too young to have a boyfriend and she better not have one! The girl was devastated. Her mother was not trustworthy. She continuously used the girl's own innocent words against her whenever the mother needed ammunition against her daughter. This mother created serious trust issues. Is there any wonder why children turn away from their parents and go to their friends instead?

Teenagers trust their parents to keep them out of harm's way. Years ago, when a young couple were found to be sexually active, the parents and their clergy might threaten them with eternal damnation if they didn't marry. Because the young people feared for their eternal souls and wanted to make things right, they married. That was not always the right choice, but many times, parents didn't want to suffer the embarrassment of a scandal. Oftentimes, years later, the entire family would suffer the pain and heartache of a bitter divorce because of the selfish advice of the parents from the very beginning.

As parents, we need to keep our children's best interest at heart, not our own. We have the ability to see further into the future than our children. We need to love them enough to make the hard decisions based on their good. We might not always be popular at the moment we put our foot down during a difficult decision, but in time, they will be grateful.

Trust is so valuable. Our child's trust will decrease his or her chance of getting into grave sin. Please, give your children that place to come to when they need help. When they are in trouble, they don't need to be afraid—they need the love and security of a parent, one that they trust to care for them and be that champion in their young lives.

Beloved, we cannot be so naïve as to think that childhood issues stop at childhood. We walk into adulthood with those CDs still playing, and our own past experiences speak loudly to us so that we can carry mistrust with us into adulthood.

The pillar of trust will always operate in our lives no matter how old we are or how successful we become. We might not believe in gravity, but it still operates in our lives every day. The same goes for the pillar of trust. We might not believe it, but it is still working in our lives every day. It not only operates every day in our lives, but it follows us as we mature.

Little did I know, as a teenager, that the pillar of trust of my parents' home would follow me into my marriage. When I was sixteen, my parents almost went through a divorce, and my dad, whom I adored, made some really foolish choices. I lost my trust in men, "knowing" all men will make the same foolish choices. I reasoned that men could not be trusted.

I went limping into my marriage with Dennis knowing that he could not be trusted. My thinking was clear and based on experience. The problem was that I didn't know I felt this way until Dennis and I hit a rough patch. Then it all came pouring out of me. Poor Dennis—he was set up in the beginning and didn't even know it. I didn't know it, either. I made him pay the price for my father, and I couldn't help it—it was the song playing on my CD, and I danced to the music I heard. Beloved, how we live our lives as husband and wife affects our children. Whether we want it to or not, it will.

A wise woman once told me that the only real truth is God's Truth. I haven't forgotten that. All truth must be measured by God's Word—it is a ruler that never changes. But we all have our own truth that we live by daily, and since we will be talking a great deal about the difference between *true* and *truth* in the next couple of chapters, let's clarify it right now.

Let's say we need to be at work at 8 a.m. We forget to set our alarm clock, and we get up at 7:30 a.m. We shower, jump in the car, and hope for a green light. While en route to the job, we get behind a street sweeper, and it puts us even further behind our schedule. When we get to the office, we tell our boss how we were behind the street sweeper and that is why we're late. While that is technically true, the truth is we didn't get out of bed on time. Therefore, the truth is we were late not because of the street sweeper, but because we didn't get up on time.

Children need to be taught early in their childhood the difference between what is true and what is truth. Usually, the truth is preferred over what is merely true, but as parents, we don't need to communicate hard-core truths about our lives with our children. They are children, and sometimes they just can't handle the truth.

Please, use some wisdom and common sense when giving them sensitive information. While it might be true that a couple is going to counseling, their children don't need to know the truth is that Daddy is a man who likes to grope his secretary. They are only little children. Give them a break when it comes to adult issues, and give them what is true, and save the truth for the teaching moments that will ensure their success as adults.

Since we have covered *true* and *truth*, let us now clarify what it means to lie. I know we don't think we need to explain what it means to lie, but I beg to differ. Many people lie just as a course of conversation. People don't even recognize the fact that they lie more than once on a daily basis.

One of the reasons I love having Micah around so much is that he is so truthful. We had an elderly gentleman over for dinner one night while Micah was at our home. Micah intently stared at our friend, then very politely said, "You know, you are old." Indeed, our friend was old. It was truth, and Micah felt like sharing.

Just because we don't lie, we are not to be unnecessarily cruel, either. Did your mom ever tell you that if you can't say anything nice about someone, don't say anything at all? That is wise advice.

Why is lying so bad? Because the basis of trust is truth. When we tell our children the truth, they know they can trust us. If we tell them we are going to do something when they are children, they will wait for it to happen. Children know that parents aren't supposed to lie to them. That is why in the beginning of their lives, all children trust their parents, unless they learn they cannot.

I have been giving a lot of thought lately to preteens and teens who join gangs that engage in illegal and/or immoral activity. What draw do these groups have on those kids? I believe it is largely because the gangs prove they can be trusted. These gangs live by a code, they have each other's back, and they prove their loyalty to each other no matter what happens. On the flip side, if they betray the gang, they will be met with a severe punishment. But even in punishment, they believe that they will be true to their word because they have proved their word to be good in the past.

In every city, large and small, in this great country we live in, there are such gangs. Some are more open than others; many live in the shadows, conducting their business in the dead of night. We have come to find out that even in the town we live in, there are several gangs that terrorize our neighborhoods. We don't live in New York or Los Angeles. We live in a small city, yet these kinds of activities have found a life and are thriving. Why? Because every day of the week, there are children who are disappointed by the adults in their lives or tossed aside by those who are supposed to love them and protect them.

An increasing number of kids are left to fend for themselves, left alone most days and some nights, and forced to make adult decisions when oftentimes, they haven't even reached middle school. Some kids are lied to by parents, grandparents, clergy, and teachers every day of their lives, telling them one thing, but doing another. Is it any wonder these kids have serious trust issues? I am not talking about kids born to drug-addicted, alcoholic parents or kids who live on the streets. I'm talking about kids born to so-called good homes, whose parents attend church or temple weekly. Kids need people in their lives they can trust.

Parents are failing their children every day because one or more of the pillars of parenting have been broken. Trust is one of those pillars. While it is devastatingly easily broken, it is not as easily repaired.

Many parents today are breaking their promises to their children on a daily basis by lying to them, breaking down the pillar of trust, and never realizing it. Kids' lives are being filled with promises that are frequently and easily broken. Some reason incorrectly that kids are only kids, and they will get over it. That kind of reasoning is dead wrong.

When a child is young, a parent may tell the child that the parent will do something with or for the child. It's imperative that the parent follows through with his or her commitment. Perhaps the child was promised a trip to the store or a grand summer vacation—make it happen. Even a promise to read a story at the end of the night is a promise that should be kept.

Promises are not only for rewards. Promises are also made when pledging punishments. When the child is misbehaving and promised a time-out but never receives it, that is a broken promise. When a child is told he will go without dessert for not eating his vegetables and yet is given ice cream before bed, that's a promise broken. Promises made and then broken equal a broken trust every time.

These parents' words and actions are saying, "Whatever you do, don't trust me, because I can't be trusted." Unfortunately, with years of practice, these parents can become master liars and not even know it.

Beloved, this is where the rubber meets the road when we talk about parents and trust. It starts out so small, so minute that if we weren't looking for it, we would never even notice.

We feel as parents that we have the right to change our minds, and we do. But once we tell a child we are going to do something, we'd better have a really good reason when we don't follow through. Our word with our children is our bond. They measure our character by whether we keep our word to them or not. They measure their trust in us by the same yardstick.

We cannot talk about the issue of trust without talking about where the issues usually originate: in toddlers. Have you noticed that in the days that we are living in, toddlers are frequently smarter than the parents? How many times have you heard a parent in the store give his or her child an ultimatum, then start counting? I just cringe. Why is the parent counting? Because he or she is getting ready to lie. The parent doesn't mean what he or she says, and sadly, the child knows too well that at ten . . . ten and a half . . . nothing will happen.

The child just waits the parent out. Eleven . . . twelve . . . the child waits. And sure enough, the parents will modify their "request" or most likely just give up.

Now the child is free to do whatever it is he or she intended to do originally. Even as a toddler, the child knows his or her parents are not trustworthy. That is why so many toddlers run their homes— they know there will be no consequences for bad behavior. They have learned to count and know that the numbers can go on, but their parents will wear out. It is at this point that they can trust their parents to not be trustworthy when it really counts.

I believe in saying please when I make a request—manners are important. But don't confuse my manners with weakness. Too many parents are pleading with their children to comply with even the simplest of requests; this is why their children lack respect for them.

When a parent doesn't deliver discipline when promised, the child loses respect for that parent's word. When a parent's word is worth nothing, the child doesn't trust the parent for anything. When a child learns he or she cannot trust his or her parents, the parents' word becomes empty. The children take charge, and the household goes to hell in a handbasket, literally.

At the toddler stage is when I can predict with some clarity what will become of a child in his or her teens—yes, as a toddler. By the time a child is three years old, the child cannot put it into words, but knows if he or she can trust his or her parents or not. Once a child knows that a parent can't be trusted, the child will use that to his or her advantage every time.

Many times when a child refuses to do something, the child is merely testing the waters, trying to see what he or she can get by with at any given time. And while children are constantly learning and growing, they should not be trying their parents every day until they are grown!

If a child consistently says NO and consistently misbehaves, it is because the child knows that his or her parents will cave in and give the child exactly what he or she wants. The child knows what will happen if he or she keeps trying the parents: The parents will give in no matter the child's behavior or demands. The child knows it and expects it every time. This is why consistency and trust at three will give you rest when the child is thirteen.

If our child knows going into the teen years that he or she can trust us to always do what we promise, our child will understand that we will follow through with our word. The child trusts us to keep our promises, whether it is giving rewards or meting out punishments. Children better understand and adhere to boundaries that we, the parents, have set when they know our word is good and that we can be trusted.

When parents consistently keep their word, they can be trusted when it comes to any life decision, big or small. Many parents have not been taught about instilling trust in their children, so parents never give a thought to the pillar of trust when they are raising their children. Yet, as we learn about the consequences and benefits of trust, we understand a child's whole life depends on the parents' keeping that pillar strong. Children respect adults they know will always tell them the truth. Respect from a teenager is huge.

When I taught school, I would make myself very clear at the beginning of the year. I would tell the students what I expected, and then I would explain to them the consequences for disobedience. Many children were accustomed to their parents' not being consistent with them; those children didn't believe me when I told them the consequences for not following through with an assignment, for talking in class, for showing disrespect, for disobeying, and so on. However, the first time someone missed an assignment or misbehaved, I would immediately follow through with my discipline plan.

Many times, I had to keep a straight face when I saw the look of shock and unbelief on the students' faces as I gave out my discipline. In many cases, the student had never had anyone in his or her life who immediately kept all his promises. What was even worse was the look on the parents' faces. How dare I give any sort of discipline to little Johnny or Susie!

Even though the parents knew the discipline plan at the beginning of the year, because they were not used to keeping their own promises, they were shocked that I planned to keep mine. I never backed down. I am blessed to say that every year, I earned the respect of parents and students alike. I was fair, but I was tough. Month after month, without fail, parents would come to my desk asking how I got their child to behave when they couldn't even get their child to be civil to them. My response was always the same: "They trust me to do what I say I am going to do, and I never make an idle threat."

I always weighed my words carefully, in the classroom as well as in my own home. If I promised I was going to do something, I did it, no matter the cost. My word had to be true, no matter what. My word was my currency, and I traded on that currency every day.

If I promised my sons we were going to the store, we went. I don't care if it is raining; a promise is a promise. Children need to know they are safe, and part of being safe is knowing you can trust someone, no matter what happens. You know you are loved when someone keeps his or her promises, even to the person's own hurt.

Beloved, it is essential that we see how all the pillars of parenting work together to keep a house strong and in balance. Without one, the house will lean too far to one side, or fall altogether.

Too many children today are out of control because their parents say they are going to do something, but they don't follow through. Parents make promises of grounding their teen for weeks, but never follow through. They promise consequences they have no intentions of keeping. They promise rewards they know they can't afford. These parents have no clue about consistency, trust, or discipline. Consequently, their households are in constant turmoil, and the parents are clueless.

I was in 4-H one year and, because we lived on a farm, my grandpa wanted us to show sheep. So my brothers and I all took our turn showing sheep. My grandpa was so proud. Please remember that I wasn't a tomboy—I was not enthusiastic about the out-of-doors at all. Deep down, I didn't want to show sheep, but I wanted to please my grandpa, so I did it.

In my young and shallow observation, sheep were smelly, dirty, nasty little creatures. A sheep was chosen for me. I didn't train it to do anything. I spent little time with my sheep. I fed it when I had to, but most times, my grandpa did the feeding, the cleaning, and the corralling. I just did what I had to do to get by concerning that sheep. I didn't raise the sheep; my grandpa did.

However, when it came time to show the sheep, my grandpa was well over the 4-H age, so I had to show my own sheep. It was all me—I was right out front in the show ring with my sheep.

I was terrified of this animal! I had spent no time with it; it didn't trust me, and I didn't trust it. We were strangers to each other. I would try to make it stand to the left, and it would go to the right. I tried to get it to put its chin up for the judges, and it balked. Frozen in fear, I jumped back, terrified, embarrassed, and ready for the experience to end.

It was obvious to anyone who knew sheep that I had no clue what to do, and neither did the sheep. Would you be surprised to know that I didn't do well in the 4-H show? The law of trust definitely applies to animals, too!

Unfortunately, there are some parents who spend no time with their children, but let everyone else watch them, feed them, and raise them. No adult in their life teaches them; the TV becomes these children's best friend. A box filled with other people's morals, convictions, and sick sense of humor feeds these parents' children. What do you think will happen when they get into the arena of teenage life? The same thing that happened to me and the sheep—total disaster!

Trust is something that doesn't happen overnight. It is a foundational truth of successful parenting. Built day by day, word upon word, tried in the fiery furnace of life, trust will walk out intact every time.

I love to bake, and I love to come up with my own recipes. Sometimes they are fabulous, and sometimes they are less than acceptable. Our sons are used to being honest with me—it's no big deal. However, our precious daughter-in-law Amber did not want to hurt my feelings when I asked her what she thought of a particular dish I had made. I knew by the look on her face she didn't love it, but I wasn't sure what she was thinking. She just smiled and nodded her head when I asked if she liked it. I couldn't get a straight answer out of this girl for love or money. Then I looked at her and said, "If you don't like it, you better tell me now, or I will make it for you over and over forever." She looked at me, still not quite sure if she could be totally honest, and smiled, and I egged her on. "Would you want to eat this again?"

She finally broke, "No."

"There! How easy was that?" I laughed. So did she.

Still, for a season, she was timid. But with time, as our relationship grew, she found she was totally safe with our family and could be totally honest without fear of reproach or retribution.

She really became quite a chatterbox of truth! I so love her for that. I am so thankful for the level of trust we have with our daughters-in-law and our sons. None of us are perfect, but with every passing day, we do our best to keep our word to each other, hold each other up as a priority, and love each other enough to be gently truthful. Jesus asked this question:

For which of you, intending to build a tower, sitteth not down first, and **count**eth the **cost**, whether he have sufficient to finish it?

Luke 14:28 (emphasis added)

Before something comes out of our mouths, we better count the cost. If we say we are going to ground our child for a year (and I never recommend this), we better be prepared to be in our home with our child for an entire year. (Now you know why I don't recommend this!) If we promise a new car to our son or daughter, we better have the finances to pay for it. If we promise a new puppy, we need to have a plan in place because we are going to have a new puppy! We go back to demonstration. We are building trust with our children through our actions. Words are empty without the actions to back them up. It is the action regarding those words that will build trust.

Trust in a relationship never stops being important. The foundation of a home is stabilized and supported by pillars and is filled with many rooms. With every new generation, we add more rooms. A wise man builds his house on a solid foundation, but he doesn't stop there. Every floor, every room needs to be formed with the cement of trust.

Beloved, there is a quiet safety in being able to trust someone. When we know we can depend on someone to always be true to his or her word, we will literally trust the person with our lives. And, Dear One, our children should be able to trust us with their lives. After all, that is our responsibility, right?

The Fifth Pillar

The Pillar of the Tongue

Death and life are in the power of the tongue: and they that love it shall eat the fruit thereof.

Proverbs 18:21

For verily I say unto you, That whosoever shall say unto this mountain, Be thou removed, and be thou cast into the sea; and shall not doubt in his heart, but shall believe that those things which he saith shall come to pass; he shall have whatsoever he saith.

Mark 11:23

My tongue shall speak of thy word: for all thy commandments are righteousness.

Psalm 119:172

If any man among you seem to be religious, and brid-
leth not his tongue, but deceiveth his own heart, this
man's religion is vain.

James 1:26

OUR TONGUE IS A small part of our body, yet with this small muscle, we enable or crush our children every day. If our tongue is loose, then it will be responsible for a big part of our children's lack of success as teenagers and young adults.

We are the artists of their lives, and we form every brush stroke they hear with our tongues. What kind of picture are we painting of their future—a bright one where they can be and do anything they want, or a bleak one rifled with limitations and failures? It is up to us. Remember, they are trusting us to do the right thing. They also trust us to say the right thing.

Listen sometime to what parents say about their children. And let's listen to what we say about our own children, as well. Have you heard this before: "Sticks and stones can break your bones, but words will never hurt you"? That statement is a lie. We all know that words hurt. Ask anyone who has a sharp-tongued spouse.

Words hurt more than sticks and stones ever will. If we are hit with a stick, it will hurt, maybe bruise, but the wound will heal in about a week. But if we hear words spoken about us, they can hurt for our entire lifetime. Words get into our spirit and into our CD, and we replay them repeatedly for years to come.

Our children's CD is playing what we have said about them. We must be in a listening mode not only when we talk to our children, but when we talk about them to others. What are we saying? Are we telling others what screwups our children are? Are we playing the comparing game—my child is worse than yours? Or are we our children's own personal cheerleader, focusing on their successes and victories? People don't need to know the mistakes our children make. It is none of their business. We need to stop sharing our children's failures and start applauding their accomplishments. Whether they are big or small, we need to be rehearsing them to all who will listen.

Recently, I lost sixty-seven pounds. I went from a size twenty to a size ten! The beginning of my journey started at this pillar. God helped me see that what I believed to be true about myself because of what was spoken about me as a child was not the truth. Words like, "You will always be heavy. It's in your genes," or, "You should have," or, "No matter what you do, you will always have fat thighs." Ouch! Or my personal favorite, the absence of affirming words. My parents never called me ugly, but they never said I was pretty, either. As a young girl, if no one calls you pretty, you will perceive the truth is that you are ugly.

Remember the difference between *true* and *truth*. Some words spoken might be true to an extent, but they are not the truth! I had to go back to my source and see what God said about me. And I found He only spoke well about me. So I went back to those lies that I had believed about myself, and I changed them into words of life. Words ruined my life! Now it was God's words about me that would save it. I just had to refuse the lie and believe the truth. Beloved, words have power.

Because our passionate ministry is to families, I tend to listen to people with children everywhere I go. I am not saying I eavesdrop, but I might linger a while at a counter to hear a complete conversation. Smile!

All too often, I hear parents saying things to their children that I know for sure will be playing on their CDs for the rest of their lives. I've heard parents call their children dumb or tell them they should be glad they are cute because they are too stupid to succeed in life on their brains. Ouch! These words are all permanently lodged in children's hearts until they are healed by God.

These children reason that their parents said it, so it must be true. The children store it away for another time, and the enemy uses such words as fuel to be the accuser of the brethren at a later time when they are struggling teens or weary adults. At critical times of their lives, their CDs play the words back for them to hear about themselves. And because it is on their CDs, they believe it to be truth about them. Beloved, God says nothing but good about us; why should we ever believe anything else?

Children hear all of their lives what their parents' expectations, dreams, and hopes are for them. This is part of that CD collection that they keep and play for a reference in their future. When in doubt about what to do or what to think about themselves, they go to that CD. The words on that CD have power. Children, without consciously doing it, will live up to or live down to everything they have ever heard about themselves. It will become who they are—their reality. Hopefully, their parents knew enough to speak life into them, but all too often, that is not the case.

How many of us know children in a home where the parents say things to their children that don't line up with the Word? They tell them they are losers, troublemakers, fat, ugly, stupid, airheads, clumsy, or a million other horrible words. What are children supposed to do with those words? They can't call their parents liars, so they take ownership of their parents' words and let those words shape who they are.

It is up to us, as parents, to change our talk and shape our children's lives for the better. This can only come through listening to wisdom and following after truth—the kind of truth that sets you free, makes crooked paths straight, and opens prison bars.

Make no mistake, these children are in prison. Sadly, it is a comfortable cell. It's the one they grew up living in, one that is familiar, a cell that their parents' words created. Built over years of their lives, word upon word, the cell was completed. And word upon word, the very cell can be destroyed. But someone must make the effort. Prison breaks are not easy. Prisons were made to keep people in for a reason, but, my beloved, many people have broken out of this prison of words, and we can break out, too. We can all be free from the words that held us captive.

When our children were young, I had read enough of the Bible and listened to enough learned men and women of God to know that words have more power than people give them credit for possessing. So I began to change how I talked to and about my own sons. Even when they were not in the same room with me, I spoke to others about them what I would want my boys to hear about themselves.

If they didn't understand something, I would not try to use the words "ignorant" or "stupid." When they made a mistake, I tried to stop making it the end of the world. When they fell short of what I wanted or expected, I didn't tell everyone I knew what had happened.

This had some unexpected results in my own families. My own mother thought it ludicrous to not say anything negative about my children as if they were perfect! My brother told me that I thought my children were better than his and was quite offended. We had the same reaction in Dennis's family, but we were undaunted. It doesn't matter who agrees or disagrees with us; when we know the right thing to do, we must do it.

Dennis is a man of very few words, so it wasn't hard for him not to say anything negative. But for me, a woman of a million words, I had undertaken a task that was *almost* too large. You see, I still had my CD playing in my head, so I had to combat negative words from all sides. We had to change what we knew to be true into what was actually the truth. I know it sounds easy, but, Beloved, I can't lie; it was difficult.

I have to admit, I failed miserably sometimes. I missed the mark on more than one occasion, going back to using my old negative words. But I never gave up. I kept speaking words of kindness, words of optimism, words of hope, words of encouragement, words of greatness, and words of life over all of my sons. I replaced the words I had been using with words that would affect them not only in the present time, but in their future. They were special, and they needed to know that every day of their lives.

There were times when we needed to discipline the boys for wrong behavior. But it didn't change what we said about them. It didn't change what we thought about them. Don't ever sugarcoat sin. Sin is to be brought out in the open, dealt with, repented from, and never brought up again. That is what we did. We didn't stop and make a monument to the problem; we kept going on the road to successful family living, one word at a time.

We used this pillar in everything we did—our marriage, our children, our finances, everything. Now, instead of saying we didn't have the money to buy something, we would say we hadn't budgeted for it that week. Instead of complaining because something wasn't going the way we wanted, we simply said it would turn around, stood on our faith in God, and went on speaking words of life. Our marriage began to turn around, our children had a better outlook, even our finances took off because we'd hit on a secret to living a successful life.

Our words had the power of life and death, and we had chosen life. We chose wisely, and therefore, we began to reap the benefits of that wisdom—namely, peace, joy, and victory in every aspect of our lives.

It is frightening the number of parents who don't know anything about this pillar of parenting. They speak any old way to their spouse and their children. They use words as weapons, taking off the heads of the very ones they have been given to love by speaking words of death and destruction over their marriage, over the children, and over the family. These words, when given a voice, will take on a life of their own.

Children who never hear affirming words don't know their own possibilities. They have no idea they can be great leaders, great inventors, great teachers, great fathers, great husbands, or great wives. They never hear these words spoken about them. Yet the parents expect great things from them. How could this possibly happen? Why do parents raise children without hope or affirmation, without confidence or encouragement, without self-worth or self-esteem, and expect them to become remarkable adults?

We prophesy our children's future every day. Which words would you like to have fulfilled in your child's life?

- You will never . . .
- You're the best!
- You can't . . .
- You can do it!
- You're too stupid to . . .
- You are so clever!

- Your choices are always wrong.
- You made a good choice today when you . . .
- You won't . . .
- You are capable of greatness!
- You never . . .
- You are beautiful!

You get the picture. I could literally go on for pages.

We need to realize the kind of power that we, as parents, hold in our mouths. The power to lift up or tear down, the power to make great or belittle, the ability to empower dreams or crush them, the power to launch visions or squash hope.

We have the responsibility to change what we say and change how we handle our speech. There are no more excuses for the hurtful words we use. We are responsible for everything that comes out of our mouths. What words will we use? I pray we all choose words that affirm—words that encourage our children's dreams and aspirations, words that give them wings. It is our choice. We are the parents, and they will believe whatever we say about them. Beloved, we must choose what we say wisely—our children's lives depend on it.

The Sixth Pillar

The Pillar of Self-Control

This I say then, Walk in the Spirit, and ye shall not fulfil the lust of the flesh. For the flesh lusteth against the Spirit, and the Spirit against the flesh: and these are contrary the one to the other: so that ye cannot do the things that ye would. But if ye be led of the Spirit, ye are not under the law. Now the works of the flesh are manifest, which are these; Adultery, fornication, uncleanness, lasciviousness, idolatry, witchcraft, hatred, variance, emulations, wrath, strife, seditions, heresies, envyings, murders, drunkenness, revellings, and such like: of the which I tell you before, as I have also told you in time past, that they which do such things shall not inherit the kingdom of God. But the fruit of the Spirit is love, joy, peace, longsuffering, gentleness, goodness, faith, meekness, temperance: against such there is no law. And they that are Christ's have crucified the flesh with the affections and lusts. If we live in the Spirit, let us also walk in the Spirit.

Galatians 5:16-25

GALATIANS 5:16-25 IS ALL about fruit. These nine fruits are used as an illustration to show the level of maturity of the believer, which includes the quality of our character and the extent to which we are willing to put down our flesh and pick up the character of God. The nine fruits of the Spirit are: love, joy, peace, longsuffering, kindness, goodness, faithfulness, gentleness, and self-control. It goes without saying that we should be working daily on growing these nine fruits in our own lives. And while all are ultra-important to our Christian walk, it is the last fruit in the list of nine, self-control, that is an important pillar in raising wildly successful children.

Think of self-control as personal responsibility and boundaries. When we have an awareness of personal responsibility and knowledge of our own boundaries, we automatically become accountable for our own lives. We know how far we can legitimately go in society without crossing the line of what is fair and decent. Our focus is off of what others are doing and on our own behavior. We become our own police force, if you will. Fences make good neighbors, and boundaries and personal responsibility make great spouses, employees, leaders, and world citizens.

Now we know why self-control is such an important pillar. Successful children become successful adults who have the opportunity to impact their community and their world for good. You cannot do that (consistently) if you lack self-control.

We all know people we consider out of control, people who lack even the smallest of impulse control. I was talking to one of my precious spiritual daughters and going over the pillar of self-control with her. She told me about her childhood and how her father would drive ninety miles an hour down the highway when he was angry. She knew how he drove because he did so with his wife and small children in the car with him. She started talking about her parents' lack of self-control as she was growing up and began relating it to her own lack of self-control in some areas of her adult life.

By her own admission, her temper sometimes had control of her, not the other way around. It wasn't until she had a child of her own that she saw her temper for what it was and determined in her heart that she would not let her daughter go down the same path that she had walked. She owned her behavior, repented, and asked God to help her gain control of her temper. Now she stops when she starts to get mad about circumstances and situations around her. If she slips, she apologizes to her daughter and accepts responsibility for her actions. Her daughter has something valuable—a parent who accepts responsibility for her own actions and demonstrates that character to her. This child is assured a valuable harvest of the fruit of self-control in her adult life.

We live in a world of excess. Perhaps that is why self-control is something that many young children don't know exists. Just glance into the average child's room—it is filled to the brim with toys, stuffed animals, and video games galore. The child has enough toys for a lifetime, and he is only a toddler. At this stage in life, is it the child who is having trouble with his problems of self-control, or is it the parents? A toddler can't go to the mall and buy everything he sees. Someone must take ownership of this problem.

I remember being told as a child, "Money doesn't grow on trees." I have to admit, there were times when I looked for that elusive money tree when I was a child, but it was not to be found. Now I know what that generation was trying to say: "You can't spend what you don't have." Seems simple enough, right? Then why are we, as a nation, in so much debt? Even our government is in debt. We have no self-control when it comes to spending. It is safe to say, as a nation and a people, that when it comes to debt, we are out of control!

It seems Dave Ramsey spends much of his airtime telling people to not spend what they don't have. You would think we would know that, but we were raised by a generation of parents who stopped using cash and started using plastic. Today we are, for the most part, a cashless society. The problem is that we are really cashless and are putting on a credit card purchases we don't have the money to cover. This really just enforces why our pillar of self-control is such an important one. Money problems are said to be the number one reason for divorce. When we demonstrate to our children that we exercise personal responsibility and boundaries when it comes to finances, we are infinitely boosting their chances of having and keeping a happy marriage.

Let's go back to this toddler. Having too much is not always a blessing. It opens the door to that part of us that is never fulfilled. The flesh always wants more. Even as a child, our flesh cries out for more—it is never satisfied. Our responsibility as parents is to teach our child what *enough* means and to know the difference between needs and wants. While God supplies all our needs and even our desires, we don't need everything we see. That is called greed.

Children should be full of gratitude and thankfulness for even the smallest of gifts. Years ago, a couple in our church gave our son Mathew a bag of army men. He thanked them repeatedly and hurried to show his brothers, who never once said, "What about me?" His brothers shared in his joy with great enthusiasm. This couple commented for months on how happy Mathew was with the smallest gesture on their part, and how they wished they had been able to give something to the other boys. But they did! They gave Mathew's brothers the opportunity to be happy and joyous for someone else—to not be selfish and greedy. They passed with flying colors, which they did in most every circumstance.

Because we lived on such a limited budget when our children were young, we didn't shower them with gifts upon every trip to the store. They received presents on their birthdays, Easter,

Christmas, and the occasional blessing. We practiced sharing early, and an attitude of gratitude was always recognized and praised. Because of our budget, shoes were bought when school started and again around Easter. One year, Timothy was about six, and a store at the mall was going out of business. I happened to find name brand shoes at a fourth of the cost. Everyone got shoes. But because Timothy's size had a larger inventory, his size shoes were marked down even lower. We were able to get Timothy two pairs instead of one. Our boys did not complain or feel slighted; they gathered around Timothy and celebrated! It was one of the most joyous times in my life. I saw such fruit from these small boys that I cried. No selfishness, no greed, just joy at the blessing God had given their brother. This scene was repeated over and over in our sons' lives.

One of the secrets we practiced was the pillar of self-control. Our boys were taught they were not the center of the universe. They were taught personal responsibility, respect, and boundaries. They shared almost everything. They had one TV for their video games, and they took turns and shared. Timothy reminded me today that the year they all got their own Game Boys for Christmas, they still shared all the games, but they were still so thankful, they were giddy! We had one family TV that we all watched together. Most times, they shared rooms. We taught them that if one of them was blessed, then God would bless the others in His time, and we just need to be patient and wait.

Now, don't get me wrong—there were times when an attitude of gratitude was not displayed. But for the most part, those attitudes appeared when they were in their late teens and early twenties. In each case, I knew it was because that certain child felt entitled because we, as parents, had been too lavish with stuff and the child had come to expect it. Or, they had become adults and were employed on their own and experienced the ways of the world with all the selfishness and greed it had to offer.

In any and every case, the quickest way to stop that ugly spirit of entitlement and selfishness is to stop feeding it. Quit showering the child with stuff for stuff's sake, and the child soon will become grateful for what he or she has. If they were adults, we prayed for them, knowing we taught them better. We did not cave in to their sense of entitlement, and they soon returned to what they knew was right—most times with an apology.

I am happy to say all of that is behind us now, and we have children and grandchildren who are the personification of gratitude. But just because the boys are grown doesn't mean we have stopped teaching. We have a whole new generation that needs to learn self-control. Just this last winter, Micah willingly gave some of his favorite toys to his cousin who was a few years younger. He gave his best with a smile and never mentioned his toys again. Micah knows that God will provide what he needs in time, and if you ask him, he needs a new four-wheeler!

We need to exercise self-control in our eating, in our speech, and in our thirst for more "stuff." Let's look at the yearly sales on the day after Thanksgiving, called Black Friday.

This year, people started getting in line the Wednesday night before Thanksgiving for the sale to begin at four o'clock in the morning the Friday after Thanksgiving! A year ago, the after-Thanksgiving sales started at 6 a.m. This year, the sales started as early as 4 a.m. Amber, my daughter-in-law, said that next year, they will start at midnight! Talk about excess. When did "stuff" become so important?

Now, I ask you, what toy, gadget, article of clothing is so important that we must shove, push, stampede, fight, curse, and claw our way into a store or through an aisle at 4 a.m.? Are we so self-consumed that we have no common courtesy or self-control? Sadder still is the number of children out with their parents on these mega shopping days, learning from the pros how a lack of self-control is demonstrated.

When I was young, we never heard our mother curse. My father is a mechanic, and on the rare occasion when things fell on him, slipped out of his hand, or wouldn't come loose, we heard a stray word. But it wasn't common, and we knew better than to reproduce his expletives. When our children were young, the same principle applied.

Without self-control, our children have no boundaries or personal responsibility. Whatever they want is theirs for the taking from whomever, whenever they please. Physiologists might have a label for it in their books, but generally, children who fit this description are called bullies.

Children learn at a young age that they can bully adults into doing whatever they please as long as they are willing to yell long and loud enough. I recently saw a talk show that was highlighting a child who was out of control. The child was seen on tape using every foul word you can think of...more than one time. She was calling her parents and her sister filthy things, demanding her way and hitting anyone within reach when she didn't get what she wanted. She screamed almost constantly and demanded her way every minute of the day. I wondered, *Where did she learn this behavior, and how did she come to think it was acceptable?* Of course, the parents had a problem with the child, but it was one they created. Letting a child do what he or she wants without any personal responsibility or boundaries is akin to arming a ticking bomb. It will go off.

Beloved, this is not a pillar we want to ignore. It must be built in our children's lives and be firm. When given boundaries, a child must adhere to them or face a consequence. The same principle that applies in the previous chapters still applies here: Disobedience brings consequences, while obedience brings rewards.

A dear friend shared with me the story of her brother who had never been taught self-control. From his toddler years, he'd been given everything he wanted. He had no concept of personal responsibility. He cursed, and his parents ignored it, never trying to correct it. He was never corrected or disciplined in any way. He was never made to do chores or share in the upkeep of the family home. The parents were warned by two pastors that if the child was not made to take personal responsibility as a boy, it would result in disaster in his teen years. The parents didn't like the counsel they were given and went on the defense, quickly pointing out other children who were in need of boundaries as well. (Can you see where he learned his lack of personal responsibility?)

Time and time again, the boy got into trouble, and every time, the parents made excuses for his behavior and never made him responsible for his own actions. With each passing year, the boy became more defiant and more challenging to authority. He ruled his house—if he didn't get what he wanted, he threw a tantrum. My dear friend told me that at twenty years of age, this young man gives his parents his approved grocery and dinner list, and his mother does all of his laundry, pays all of his bills, and pays for all of his dates and his cigarettes. Sadly, this behavior will continue until this young man's parents can no longer get him out of the situations he gets into. I have said it before—for some kids, the court systems are the only place they will meet authority that they cannot bully or manipulate. Unless these parents wake up and take their own personal responsibility, that is where this young man is headed.

Beloved, do you see the urgency of the times? Many parents of this generation have raised a generation of kids with no boundaries and no personal responsibility.

My son Michael recently told me a story that made me shake my head in disbelief. He was boarding a plane and finding his seat when he heard the girl behind him using vulgar language. He said he turned around to see two girls perhaps nineteen or twenty years of age. One of the girls continued the vulgarity with no end in sight. Finally, a male flight attendant came over and asked her to quiet down and quit cursing. She became even more belligerent, picked up her cell phone, and called her father. She told her father that she was being harassed and unfairly treated, cursing the entire time. The flight attendant got the pilot, who also asked the young girl to quit cursing and told her that if she refused, she would be escorted off the plane. She continued to tell her father she was being harassed and loudly cursed everyone around her.

Michael said he was not sure what the father was saying, but she did not calm down when talking to him. She grew even more hateful. It was clear that, if she truly was talking to her father, this father was accustomed to making excuses for bad behavior on his little girl's part. This father had the authority and even the duty to calm her down and set her straight, but he did not do it.

Because this was Thanksgiving week, the plane was full of children listening to this venom. These children were held captive by the walls of this plane, yet this young woman didn't care. She had no respect for anyone of any age, something I am sure she learned early in life.

When this young woman saw that the pilot and flight attendant meant business, she stopped the profanity, but Michael said she never changed her attitude. She ceased the profanity, but worked her best the rest of the flight to make it as unpleasant as she could for everyone around her.

This was not a small child or a young teenager. This was a young woman who has the right to vote, marry, and have children. Where did she learn this behavior? Who taught her that this foul venom was acceptable?

Now, looking ahead, can you imagine marrying this girl? Can you imagine having her as a daughter-in-law or working for her or with her? Sadly, she lacked any and all self-control. Perhaps she wasn't taught self-control; perhaps she didn't think it a necessary attribute to have. Whatever the situation, this young girl will keep coming up against people wherever she goes, all because she did not learn the value of controlling herself.

Galatians 5:22 is about fruit. Fruit is used as an illustration to show the level of maturity of the believer—how good we are to others and how well we live in society. One of the fruits is self-control, which is one's ability to keep himself or herself under control in any and all kinds of circumstances.

This fruit of self-control is our thermostat—a key piece of hardware that is sorely lacking in today's society. A thermostat is an instrument for regulating the temperature of a building so that the building's temperature is maintained at the desired set position. That is essentially what self-control does in our lives. It keeps us at a constant temperature—not too hot, not too cold. But this key piece of hardware is missing in some lives, and people can become like the young girl on the plane, not monitoring her own behavior, not caring about what or who is around her, or what impact her behavior is having on other people.

A few months ago on a stormy summer day, my husband and I were at a local movie theater. The storm knocked out all of the theater's credit card machines. The line for tickets was backed up to the parking lot because people had to pay cash for their tickets or be turned away. Most people were a little aggravated because there was no shelter, and the skies were turning dark, waiting to dump heavy rains over the theater. But while the people were not happy, we all patiently awaited our turn in line. Suddenly, one man yelled for the cashiers to hurry up and screamed at the people to start moving faster in the line. Most of the people in line just stood silently. I looked questioningly at this quarrelsome man.

He looked at me and said, "Hey, I come from New York, and we wouldn't stand for this where I come from. People would not just be standing around; they would be screaming and rushing this place. People around here are just too polite."

I just smiled at him politely and continued to stand quietly in line. Can you imagine being called too polite? I wondered later, *Would people really do that over movie tickets?*

All too often, parents fail to teach the pillar of self-control to their children. Now the children and the homes are out of control, and no one knows what to do.

If we see ourselves in this picture, we need only to stop, take a breath, repent, and ask God for help. Next, we go to our children and tell them we were wrong and we are going to make things right—starting now. Then we set those boundaries and (the hard part) start demonstrating and teaching personal responsibility.

- *We are each responsible for our own emotions, our own decisions.*
- *We are not controlled by our flesh; we control our flesh.*

- *Wrong choices will bring consequences, and that is expected.*
- *We don't get what we want all of the time, and that has to be okay.*
- *We are not going to get ahead by cheating.*
- *We must all treat everyone fairly, just like we would want to be treated.*
- *We will be given boundaries in life, and we must adhere to them; they are there for our good.*

Recently, a young girl was selling Girl Scout cookies with her mother, who had left for a few minutes to use the restroom. While her mother was gone, two young women in their late teens robbed the girl of all of her cookie money. A local newsperson was on the scene after the girls were arrested and asked them why they had robbed this young child. The teenagers laughed at what they had brazenly done. They said they wanted the money to go shopping and were entitled to it simply because they wanted it! It was there, they wanted it, so they took it.

Shock ran through me. What happened to personal responsibility and self-control in our society? One of the thieves said a few days later that she didn't think she needed to be punished because they (the police) made her give the money back!

I am telling you as sure as I am living and breathing, somewhere these girls have been denied proper training. It is our parental responsibility to teach our children boundaries, responsibility, and respect. These girls were not some gang members or some drug addicts looking for their next fix. They were not homeless children looking for their next meal. These girls wanted to shop! They displayed no self-control or personal responsibility whatsoever. I can't say that I have ever heard of anyone, no matter their dire circumstances, taking Girl Scout cookie money from a small child in broad daylight. Even when caught red-handed, the girls took no responsibility and thought they deserved no punishment. They had a total lack of self-control in their lives.

Don't be lulled into a false sense of security if you have preteens. In today's society, a ten-year-old without the balance of self-control in his or her life can be just as malicious as any teenager or adult. Age means nothing anymore when dealing with personal responsibility or boundaries. What was unthinkable even ten years ago is commonplace today. Drugs and drinking are off the charts in our teens and preteens today, and sex is reported to be a commonplace activity among middle school children, even children as young as ten! These statistics are true due to the lack of boundaries, personal responsibility, and accountability.

What is to become of this generation? Kids beat each other up because they want to inflict pain for amusement—all videotaped on the Internet. Kids steal cars just to joyride around the town and shoplift from stores for the excitement—not because they are hungry or cold, but because they are bored.

As parents, we need to say, "Enough." We need to start teaching our children the pillar of self-control before it is too late. This pillar of self-control, as with all other pillars, hinges on the pillar of demonstration.

Sadly, when we watch our nightly news, we see where these children learn their behavior—the news is full of adults who lack self-control. People kill each other over traffic incidents or words spoken in anger. Parents attack and sometimes fatally injure fellow parents at children's sporting events. If we wonder where our children learn their behaviors, we need only look in the mirror.

We can't talk about self-control and not mention our nation's love of buffets. Overeating has become a national epidemic. My grandfather used to take the grandkids (then the great-grandkids) out to eat. We would always go to a buffet, and Grandpa would tell us during the meal that we needed to eat as much as we could so he could get his money's worth, which meant, even if we were full, we still needed to eat more. We were learning to be gluttons. What a poor training ground for a short, former emotional eater like me!

We need to wake up and smell the coffee (cinnamon rolls) before we lose this generation altogether. A nation that has no self-control is a nation that is doomed for self-destruction. Americans (as well as many other nations) are raising greedy, overly-indulged children who grow more unbearable with each passing year. Sadly, "self-control" is a word that is virtually outdated in our culture. We must bring this teaching back into our homes and our churches. Time is too short to sugarcoat what is happening right on our own front lawns!

Beloved, what was right as far as manners and self-control fifty years ago still applies today. Doing the right thing never goes out of style. If we want to keep our kids off the talk shows, off the nightly news, and out of prison, self-control is the key. We must teach our child the value of controlling his or her emotions, eating, and lifestyle, and we will have a child that can weather any storm with grace and dignity.

Never did Dennis and I lose one night of sleep when our children began to drive. And keep in mind that at one time in our lives, we had four young drivers. We knew they all adhered to the pillar of self-control.

Dennis especially is a great teacher when it comes to self-control. He is the epitome of grace under pressure. As Dennis gets older in the Lord and grows in wisdom, he shows even more self-control. He doesn't get frustrated easily, nor does he get bothered by big problems. He is a good man to have around at any time, but he is a great man to have around in a crisis.

The boys come to me for day-to-day counsel, but for a situation that is big, that has to do with a large sum of money, or that calls for a cool head full of common sense—they call their dad every time. I am pleased to say that all the boys learned the same self-control that Dennis modeled. A great husband is always a great father, and Dennis is both.

Today our boys are well-mannered, well-behaved, and level-headed. We raised four boys at the same time, and it wasn't easy. The pillar of self-control was invaluable in raising cool, calm, and rational boys. We didn't get it right all the time, but God is full of mercy, and we had many chances to keep working on our parenting skills. Like every other pillar, self-control takes practice, especially if the parents (like Dennis and me) are programmed with the wrong information on our CD. But don't be discouraged. God is always on our side, guaranteeing our success!

Be encouraged. If you have not been raised with the pillar of self-control, God will supply you with a model. All you need to do is ask, or perhaps just pay attention to the influence of others around us. While my grandfather was urging us to eat ourselves into obesity, my grandma was the opposite. She was all about balance. She never overate, never overindulged in anything, never got out of balance with her eating in any way. In seventy years, from her twenties to her nineties, her weight fluctuated all of ten pounds. That's why Grandma Lorene was my favorite—she wrote the book on balance. As usual, she didn't just have balance in one area; she personified balance in every area of her life. She didn't write the book on self-control; she lived it! She used to tell me stories about her life, and I would smile because I love stories of the "olden days." But many times, I think back to those stories and go, "AH! I get it!" She was teaching me about self-control. Of course, I didn't realize what a jewel she was until she was gone. It was those lessons I remember on self-control in her life that I use as a model in my own today.

Beloved, we all lack character in one point or another when dealing with the fruit of self-control. None of us have arrived. But we owe it to God, our spouses, our children, and ourselves to keep working on it. Develop those boundaries and areas of personal responsibility every day. Self-control is a fruit of the Spirit that we need to make sure is on our children's plates every day. If an apple a day keeps the doctor away, a good dose of self-control every day keeps the devil away! If we don't live in the flesh, he can't work in us.

> Walk in the Spirit, and ye shall not fulfil the lust of the flesh. For the flesh lusteth against the Spirit, and the Spirit against the flesh: and these are contrary the one to the other: so that ye cannot do the things that ye would.
>
> Galatians 5:16-17

Let us not be slack as some previous generations have been and discount the importance of self-control in our lives and in our children's lives. Somewhere there is a daughter-in-law or a son-in-law that will thank you.

The Seventh Pillar

The Pillar of Association

He that walketh with wise men shall be wise: but a companion of fools shall be destroyed.

Proverbs 13:20

Make no friendship with an angry man; and with a furious man thou shalt not go: Lest thou learn his ways, and get a snare to thy soul.

Proverbs 22:24-25

Forsake the foolish, and live; and go in the way of understanding. He that reproveth a scorner getteth to himself shame: and he that rebuketh a wicked man getteth himself a blot. Reprove not a scorner, lest he hate thee: rebuke a wise man, and he will love thee.

Proverbs 9:6-8

SHOW ME YOUR FRIENDS, and I'll show you your future.

It was with great hesitation that I included this pillar in the book. Although it has long been a pillar of parenting in many homes, I know it can be taken too far by well-meaning parents. With all things, Dear One, we need to have balance. Something I have learned as I have gotten older and have grown in wisdom is that we don't want to be ditch dwellers, going from one extreme to another. Living in ditches drives our kids crazy and far from where they need to be in life. We personally know too many parents who made the concept of association a law instead of a pillar. When it's a law, the children most always rebel and find themselves out of the will of the Father and out of touch with their families.

When put in its proper perspective, the pillar of association can and will build a child's self-worth and give the child the courage to make life-affirming decisions that prosper the child all of his or her life. We want to give them the tools to choose friends wisely.

I was praying about this chapter and thinking back on how this pillar played such a pivotal role in our sons' lives as well as our family's future. And as if to confirm the importance of association, within two days, everywhere I turned stories poured out from friends and family members near and far about how their children, cousins, brothers, sisters, and even friends would have turned out differently if they had chosen their friends with more wisdom and prudence.

One such story came when I called my phone service provider. We were talking about what I do, and he just poured out his heart about his twin brother, whom he hadn't seen in many months. They had been close all of their lives until their senior year in high school. It was then that the other brother started hanging out with a different group of friends. His life was downhill from there. The young man I was speaking with went on to a steady job and marriage. His brother, however, took a different path; he didn't hold a steady job. Instead, he chose to hang with his friends and party. The young man I spoke with said that the family thought his brother would stop hanging with his new friends after a month or two. He didn't. His full potential was never realized because of his choice of friends. Instead, he lived to party and partied to live. His family is sure that had he chosen different friends, he would not be the lost soul he is today.

When I was young, I used to listen to the older folks talk about people and what was going on in our small town. Oh, how small-town people love to talk! Time and time again, they used the same proverb: "Birds of a feather flock together." In almost every situation, the problem involved someone (especially the younger generation) who had gone down a wrong path. The person had turned from how he or she was raised, left the church, and rebelled against family ties and family values. The root of the problem was usually traced back to the friends with whom the person was involved.

The pillar of association is a tool for us to use to train our children on how to choose friends wisely. We get our blueprint for this pillar from the Word. Psalm 1:1 tells us not to take counsel from the ungodly or stand with sinners or the contemptuous. I interpret Proverbs 1:7-16 to say that if we want wisdom, we need to reverence the Lord. It says that fools despise wisdom, not reverencing God. Sinners hurt the innocent, and we should not be associated with them. Proverbs 6:12-19 proclaims that a naughty person has a stubborn, contrary, and disobedient mouth and heart. He is mischievous and starts trouble, which will come upon him quickly. It goes on to say there are six things the Lord hates, but the seventh one He intensely hates: a proud look, a lying tongue, hands that shed innocent blood, a heart that thinks up wicked imaginations, feet that are swift in running to mischief, a false witness that speaks lies, and he that causes conflict between people. I don't want to hang around people like this.

Deuteronomy 13:6-9 clearly says that anyone, including family or friends, who tries to get you to turn against God involves idolatry. Idolatry is anything that turns your heart away from the things of God. The verses say you should not hang around them or feel bad that you aren't around them.

One of the clearest Scriptures on friends is found in Proverbs 13:20: If you walk with wise men, you will be wise, but if your friends are foolish, you will meet with a tragic end.

Beloved, I believe with these Scriptures we have a very clear picture of what God expects for us to teach our children concerning their friendships. We, as their parents, need to instruct them to choose wisely when choosing a friend. Not everyone should be our friend, and that's all right.

Ah, but what about Zacchaeus? Zacchaeus was in a tree *wanting* to see Jesus. Jesus was sent to the lost. He knew Zacchaeus was ready to reject his sinful ways and follow him. He knew because there was this man up in a tree. He was desperate to see Jesus. Jesus never says no to a desperate person.

Jesus always ministered to the sinners, but he fellowshiped with his disciples. He spent his time with those he wanted to be closer with and briefly engaged the rest of the people. He really took it a step further. Jesus was very close to three, associated with eight, and endured one. Here is the foundation that the pillar of association is grounded in: **We minister to weakness, and we fellowship with strength.**

There is a difference between ministering and fellowshiping. "**Ministering**" *means giving help to someone in need.* We give help to the weak. "**Fellowshiping**" *means associating with a group of people who share common interests, goals, experiences, or views. It also means having companionship or friendly association.* We fellowship with those who are headed the same way we are headed, those who will be a blessing to us along our journey, as we will be a blessing to them also.

We will usually choose our child's playmates when they are two, but not when they are twelve. But it is at twelve when they most need our guidance when it comes to their friends. Which of us at eight or twelve had the whole world and everyone in it figured out? Beloved, we adults have a hard time choosing friends if we have not been properly taught. Yet, we leave our children to pick out their friends and rely on them to know the ones who need ministry and the ones with whom they can fellowship. If we leave the blind to lead the blind, there will be a whole lot of kids in the ditches.

If we properly understand and teach this pillar to our children, by the time they are young adults, they should have no problem knowing the difference between ministering to someone and fellowshiping with them. They will soon be making wise choices. But it's up to us to teach it.

> For a good tree bringeth not forth corrupt fruit; neither doth a corrupt tree bring forth good fruit. For every tree is known by his own fruit. For of thorns men do not gather figs, nor of a bramble bush gather they grapes. A good man out of the good treasure of his heart bringeth forth that which is good; and an evil man out of the evil treasure of his heart bringeth forth that which is evil: for of the abundance of the heart his mouth speaketh.
>
> Luke 6:43-45

No matter how we try, we cannot get good fruit from a bad tree. Jesus clearly teaches that men are known by their fruit. We do not judge the people around us, Beloved, but we are to be fruit inspectors. And where does Jesus say that we can first see if that fruit is good or not? "For of the abundance of the heart his mouth speaketh."

There it is. We listen to the mouth first. What are your child's friends saying in front of you? Usually, you can bet if they will say some off-color things in front of you, they are saying a whole lot more behind your back. What are your child's friends saying about their parents, or what are they saying to their parents? How do they talk about their teachers? How do they talk to their teachers? What do they say about other children, or what do they say to other children? If we'd learn to listen to our children's conversations, we would be in a better position to guide them wisely on their choice of friends.

In almost every verse, the Scriptures said the same thing— you become like the person you hang around with, so don't hang around foolish people. Children are very adaptable. They will act one way around their parents, one way around their grandparents, a different way around their peers, and still another way around strangers. Think of them as chameleons. They become like those they spend time with on a regular basis.

Back in the eighties, when our new pastors came to the church, our pastor's wife called everyone "Darling" or "Angel." It was only a short time, and I was using the same greetings. We left that church after many years, and I quit using those terms of endearment. Now, after being away from her for more than fifteen years, we are back together with her, and it didn't take me long! I now call everyone "Angel," even my dog!

Get a child alone, and he or she will most likely be good. Put the child with a hyper child, and he or she will usually become hyper. It usually never goes the other way. The strongest personality wins. We just got a puppy, and he is such a cuddle-bug with me all day long. When Dennis comes home, he plays with the puppy, and he becomes a hyper little dog. Association makes a difference, even in animals.

Jesus loved everyone, but was closer to some than to others. Now, we might argue it was the disciples' choice to be close to Jesus, and it was. But what was their motive? The disciples wanted to become better human beings and to become like Him. Sometimes we want to be around certain people to "get" what they have. That's what the disciples were doing—pulling the wisdom out of Jesus.

Our assistant pastors, Pastors James and Claudette, are perhaps the most godly people I have ever met. People flock to them. They are kind, loving, compassionate, merciful, intelligent, nonjudgmental, and experienced. You name the fruit of the Spirit, and they possess it! They pastored a church in New York for thirty years, so they know a thing or two about people. I do my best to be around them as much as I can because I want what they have.

All of my life, I have been known as a talker. When we were in meetings, I wanted everyone to hear what I had to say. I felt everyone would benefit from my opinions, so I almost always threw in my two cents.

After spending quality time with Pastor Claudette, I have taken up her philosophy and her mannerisms. YEAH! I am keeping my mouth shut, and if I have something to say in a meeting that would be better suited one on one, I wait. I don't grumble or complain, and I try my best to be kind to everyone. There are some other things I am still working on, but you get my drift.

A week or so ago, a woman who was new to our church came up to me and told me how she admired my quietness! Yes, I said quietness. She said she loved my gentle spirit and how I conducted myself and wanted to be around me. I am not making this up! I almost fainted! She had me until she quoted Titus 2:3 that the aged women should teach good things to the younger. My problem was she was only about five to eight years younger than I. Again, Pastor Claudette came to the rescue. She reminded me that there is no such thing as age in the Spirit, and we could be younger than someone and yet be the person's teacher. I found peace with that. Godly counsel and wisdom will bring peace every time!

Now, here is the caveat. Fifteen years ago, I was a gossip, a backbiter, envious, full of jealousy, and, we know, a rabid talker. That also describes the people I was socializing with. *Birds of a feather*...I can clearly testify to how association has affected my own life and the lives of my family members. We have learned so many lessons over the years.

Of course, we all know why I desire to hang out with Pastor Claudette; she makes me a better person. One afternoon with her, and I am good to go for a week. Pastor Claudette is a great visual of the pillar of association. I am a better person because of my relationship with her. Our children's associations should make them stronger, not weaker.

Please understand, the pillar of association is not here to inflict pain on others. It is not to separate the haves from the have-nots, nor is it here to make our children feel superior in any way.

The pillar of association exists to protect our children from the schemes of the enemy and to keep them from being distracted by drama, chaos, and sin. It exists to allow peace to reign in our lives. It is there to teach our children that, like Pastor Claudette, there are people who are there for their good; people who help us be better people. But there are also people who aren't good for us. They bring out the worst in us, and when we are around them, we fall far short of our potential.

If we cannot tell by the children's speech around us, how do we know which children are going to be ones who bring our kids higher and which ones will lead them into the ditch?

Here are some warning signs of children with whom we might want to limit our child's time:

- They consistently lie.
- They take things without permission.
- They are sneaky.
- They try to persuade your child to break your rules.

- They fight.
- They skip school.
- They are preoccupied with the opposite sex.
- They have no respect for their parents or authority in general.
- They are rude.
- They use foul language.

As you can see, this list has nothing to do with a child's social standing, color, or religion. It is strictly based on the child's character. We measure people only by their character.

Here are some things we are looking for when we are choosing the children our kids spend time with:

- They are respectful to adults.
- They try to follow the rules.
- If they get into trouble, they don't get angry.
- They are helpful.
- They are kind and considerate.
- They use manners, or even when they haven't been taught many, they try.
- They are content and satisfied, not whiney and greedy.
- They know how to share.
- They can get along with more than one child at a time.

As you can see again, this has nothing whatsoever to do with a child's social standing, color, or religion. It is strictly based on the child's character.

A person's character is not the shell that person is housed in on this earth. Some of the most godly people I have ever met ride motorcycles, have tattoos, have strange hair, are way short or way tall, are painfully thin or a little round. Some even seemed a little scary at first. But when I got past the outside and saw what their character held, I loved them.

One year, Dennis and I were chaperoning a conference for teenagers called Acquire the Fire. In my section, there was a group of kids who had mohawks, piercings, tattoos, and wild jewelry. I looked at them with great suspicion. I wondered why they were there among all the "normal" kids. I just watched them, sometimes staring, sometimes glaring.

Day after day, there they were, never being rude or disruptive, just being different. On one of the last days, there was a great worship group on stage, and I watched all the kids join in the singing. But this "special" group of kids didn't join in the singing; they started to worship—open, honest, sincere worship.

I bowed my head in shame. I had judged them without knowing them. And while we are admonished to know those who labor among us and know the fruit they bear, we are not to judge someone's heart. I had judged them as less because of how they dressed and how they looked. We don't judge the outside. We evaluate the character, looking for the good fruit. I had evaluated wrongly. They had honest hearts and good character. It was just housed in a way I didn't understand. I learned a valuable lesson that weekend—and found a daughter-in-law, but that's a story for another time!

The only way we, as parents, are going to know the truth about another child's character and see the child's fruit is to spend some time around him or her. We don't necessarily need to have the child in our home. If it is a child from church or a family friend, just observe him or her casually. If it is a child from school, talk to the teacher to get some feedback. If it is a family member, well, we probably don't need a brick to fall on us. We know how our own family acts.

A good basic ground rule is that while our children are young, we should be with them at all times when they are with their friends. After we are comfortable with the parents of our children's friends, then and only then should we leave them.

When we allow people to have influence in our children's lives, we need to know exactly what these people are demonstrating to our children. It is our responsibility as a parent to know who the people are that we allow to be involved with our children. Again, get out the inspector's uniform and start looking at fruit.

What goes on in their home when our child is there? What are they allowed to watch on TV or the computer? What kind of music do they listen to on a regular basis? What are they allowed to eat? Who else is in the house while our child is there? Again, a good basic rule is to spend time with these people. We should not leave these questions for our children to answer for us. It is our responsibility.

Let's say for argument's sake, we don't particularly care for the parents of our child's friend. If we won't spend time with the parents, our children shouldn't have to, either. After all, we know by the pillar of demonstration, a child will be what his or her parents have demonstrated.

Perhaps we do try to get to know some of the parents and discover that we have very different ideas about parenting. We don't see eye to eye with them on how they raise their children. But we do like them as people. If we still want our children to play together, then we do it at the playground or a restaurant play area, a place where we know we have the freedom and flexibility to leave when we please without a huge fuss. But we must never leave our child in their care.

When we leave our child with someone, we are literally giving that person jurisdiction over our child. Jurisdiction means "the power, right, or authority to interpret and apply the law," meaning that person can interpret how to parent our child without our permission. Beloved, if we don't like the way the person parents his or her child, why would we give that person total authority over ours?

The truth is that bad company does and will always corrupt good morals. And every person in our life is not necessarily always good for us. It makes no difference if it is an associate, a friend, or even our family. Just because we know someone, we don't have to fellowship with that person, nor do we have to become lifelong friends. If someone is affecting our child (or us) for the worse, no matter who he or she is, that person must be removed from our lives quickly.

Dennis and I did that many times in our own lives and for our children. We watched as family members struggled with harmful situations. We knew we could not expose our children or ourselves to those destructive situations, so we made the difficult decision to go our separate ways. It was hard at first. But I know in one instance after we distanced ourselves from a certain relative, our children became closer, and our home became calmer. I remember the day I stopped and thought, *Wow, I know what peace feels like for the first time in a long time.*

Beloved, when talking about association, the subject of family is the hardest one to negotiate. A friend of a friend was in a similar situation recently. Her in-laws were in town and wanted to babysit the grandkids. The problem was that the grandparents didn't respect the parents' rules about anything, and they said so freely, openly defying the parents' authority in front of the children.

Angel, I don't care who it is—our mother or our mother-in-law, sister, or aunt—we are the authority in our homes, and anyone who tells our children any different has lost the privilege of being in our child's life for a season. I know that sounds harsh, but remember, our associations should make us better people. How can our children be better when they are being taught to disrespect their parents or even to rebel against our rules? We should have no reservations with making our boundaries plain and following through with our consequences. Our children's lives are at stake.

The truth is that as adults, we should be ever diligent when it comes to the enemy and how he uses people to distract and defeat us. When the issue of associating with friends and family members comes up, even the strongest of believers lose their focus and become confused.

The enemy comes to kill, steal, and destroy our lives and what God has planned for us now and in the future. Too many times, people come into our lives (or are already there), and they do nothing more than distract us from our purpose and keep us in such drama that we can't even think straight. We often tell our kids to focus, but it is difficult to focus in the midst of drama. That is another foundation of the pillar of association—cut the drama.

We have a very real enemy that is after our children and their future. If we are not diligent when it comes to what our children do and whom they do it with, who will govern them? And if we are not watching over their associations, we will all pay the price.

I was talking to Tiffany (my daughter-in-law) today, and we were talking about a family that was full of drama. Every day something new and more horrible than the day before was happening in this family. The parents didn't feel it was their responsibility to teach their children how to choose friends. And probably if the truth be told, the associations the parents had were no better. So the pillar of demonstration kicks in, and all hell breaks loose. Consequently, the children are now in their early twenties, and the drama in their house has escalated to a level of cosmic proportions. We stopped for a minute and reflected on our immediate family. Praise God, we couldn't find one place where we had any drama at all. The pillar of association was holding its place well in our home.

Beloved, that is why we have to stay away from the people in our lives who are causing drama every five minutes. It is not healthy. It keeps us off task and puts us in a constant state of chaos. Drama will erode our peace and our joy.

We all know teenagers are prone to drama, given all those hormones running through them. But when our teenager's friend is a drama magnet, we need to take notice and begin some strong intervention. If not, we can be sure that somewhere, somehow our teenagers are going to be sucked in.

There was a sweet young woman in our neighborhood. She loved God and loved to be around His people. This girl had a great future. She met a boy while in high school whose life and family were full of drama. He was a free-spirited young man who took her attention off of the things of God and introduced her to more worldly activities. She started to rebel at home and lost focus at school. So much was going on with her and her boyfriend, it was like a soap opera. It wasn't long before this beautiful girl was pregnant. She left school, and her whole family left the church.

Her parents never believed this could happen to their family. They didn't like the boy, but because they didn't want their daughter, who was already rebellious, to rebel further, they ignored the relationship. The family was shattered. The young girl and the boy got married, had three children, and then divorced. A few years later, she lost all three children to a horrible tragedy.

She spent ten more years going from one hell to another. Angel, she was off the highway that God had planned for her.

Please remember, God allows U-turns at every stop, but we have to have the wisdom and the desire to make those U-turns. She spent more than twenty years in the wilderness. It didn't have to be that way. But like a snowball, once the drama has a family upside down, the problems just escalate.

Our family has had some experience in this area. Years ago, Mathew started dating a nice Christian girl. It was his first serious girlfriend, and he was head over heels in love. He brought her to our home to meet us, and I invited her to go to the store with me. Within five minutes, I knew this was not the girl for my son. She was shallow and more self-absorbed than the usual teenager. I won't go into the whole story, but when we felt the time was right, we spoke truth to him. He did not want to hear it. He had begun to lie to us and go places that were not in his character.

We were at war with the enemy. This was our son, and we were not letting the enemy have him. The drama in our home at that time was so thick you could cut it with a knife. We didn't let up. We would not give him a free pass to a wrong relationship, a relationship we knew would ruin his life. This is how serious we must take our children's associations. Their lives depend on it.

I started asking God what to do. Finally, He spoke to my heart and told me what to pray. I called six of my closest prayer warrior friends, and we prayed and fasted for three days. Beloved, we didn't condemn this girl in our prayers. She had great ambitions. She wanted to be taken care of by a man—she wanted a man she could control physically as well as mentally. We basically asked God to give her what she wanted and to show Mathew who she really was inside. Just so you know, on the outside, she was very pretty. On the inside, not so much.

At the end of the three days, Mathew was reading her e-mail because they shared passwords with each other. He found some e-mails from an older man that were quite explicit. She had been seeing the other man almost as long as she had been seeing Mathew. Long story short, she was out of Mathew's life that day!

The rest of the story is even more interesting. After dating Mathew, this girl broke up three marriages and had a horrible reputation where she worked because she was sleeping her way to a better job. She was eventually fired from a profession she loved, losing her reputation and her livelihood in the bargain.

Remember, she professed to be a Christian. We didn't care what she said she was; we were inspecting fruit, and it was rotten. Dennis and I had tried to reason with her parents before our group began praying, but her parents refused to confront her. They seemed more concerned with hurting her feelings and driving her away than with her future. So they supported her—a choice I am sure they regretted later.

As for Mathew, he was so dejected that he went into the Air Force, which turned out to be the best thing that could have happened to him.

Beloved, all that the enemy had planned for Mathew and our family turned out for our good, which will happen for God's children who make the right choices. We know if we had not taken a stand and had allowed wrong associations to take root in Mathew's life, his life would have been less than God's best. He would have missed out on the experiences he had in the Air Force and all the maturity it brought. And that's not to mention the most important thing he would have missed—his beautiful wife and children, his very heart and greatest treasure. Mathew and his future were far too valuable to us and to the kingdom for us to just wait and see what might happen. We were the parents, and we had a responsibility to lead him the way we knew he should go. We did not negotiate with Mathew. He was a teenager. He was not aware of the ramifications of his actions, but we were. We didn't care if he liked us or not. As parents, we are not supposed to be popular; we are supposed to be vigilant. Just a note: Mathew thanked us later.

Our children do not have the ability to understand that what they do as teenagers often follows them through their lives. One slip, one wrong association, and they could lose a career choice, scholarship, marriage, family, or even their lives.

That is why it is so important for us to help them when they are choosing their friends. We need to explain why we don't want them hanging out with Johnny or Bill. What is it that they want to do with Johnny or Bill that they can't do with Fred or Mike? We need to have solid answers to their questions about why we don't want them to fellowship with that person.

But when backed into a corner, and we know the relationship is detrimental to our children, we must take a stand and make the tough choices. It is our responsibility. No, we won't be popular.

But what responsible parent is popular when his or her child is a teenager? Remember, we have a very real enemy, and he does not want our children to succeed in their Christian walk. Wrong associations have long been a staple in the devil's arsenal against our children. We must be wise to his schemes and teach our children to be wise also. We must fight to keep them from wrong associations like their lives depend on it—because they do.

I was in the grocery store one day and struck up a conversation with a sweet-looking Gator fan. We were talking about an upcoming game, and I asked him if he attended the University of Florida (UF). He lowered his head and said he was supposed to attend there that fall, but had started running with the wrong crowd and got into trouble. When this happened he lost his scholarship completely. While he was old enough to pick his own friends, I wondered if he had ever been taught which friends to choose. I decided he had not. If we give our children the tools to choose friends now, they might place those tools on the shelf for a couple of years. But never fear, they will get them out and use them when needed. Beloved, our children can't use what we don't give them.

A young man, about fourteen years old, was arrested a few years back while breaking into a house in his neighborhood. The young man had begun hanging out with another kid whose fruit was just plain bad. This kid had all ten warning signs given on the previous pages. I had spoken to the young man's mother about the friendship and voiced my concerns for her son. She wasn't worried, because teens will be teens, and boys will be boys. She wanted her son to have friends, and this kid lived close. She was sure her son would know better than to do anything stupid.

After she bailed him out of jail, he was put on probation. She then forbade him to be near this boy again, but didn't stay true to her word. Remember consistency and trust? She let him again associate with this kid. But the damage was already done. As far as I know, this young man never learned to choose his friends wisely. His life is full of wrong associations and drama.

We need to be cautious when it comes to our children's friends. Somehow, this mother thought that her son could hang out with a hoodlum and not become one. The Bible says hang out with an angry man, and you will learn his ways...and snare your own soul.

Did you know when the Secret Service does an in-depth security clearance, it checks to see who your friends are? Our government knows that you are who you hang with and even makes judgments on a person's associations. The government knows it, but we believers sometimes have a hard time accepting it.

It was God's will for our sons to join their respective branches of the service, and it has been a great blessing to them and to our family for them to serve their country. I know the enemy had many snares he wanted to use against them when it came to associations. Thankfully, we were very involved in their lives and kept driving home the price of wrong associations. Now they are grateful we were there for them.

A wise woman told me once that I didn't need fifty different friends to make me happy. Just a couple of people who are truly good friends will be more than enough for the rest of our lives. If we have one for every day of the week, we have enough. After all, if we have too many, we will be spread so thin and not have enough time for anything else, especially our family or ourselves. That would be a grave mistake. This woman knew the value of associations. She is one of the friendliest people on the face of the earth, but she chooses her close friends well. Dennis and I are blessed to be in that limited, but extraordinary, group.

Too many times, parents think their children need a dozen friends or more to be happy. This is just not true. It is we, not they, who put that kind of expectation on our kids. If our children have one or two really good friends, they are happy. Life is not a popularity contest. Our children should not be judged by how many children they have at their birthday parties. It is tough these days to find kids with extraordinary character, and yet, we want fifty for our child. Trust me, in that fifty will be some bad apples. Go for the few, and pick the best.

Contrary to popular belief, it is not he who has the most toys or the most friends who wins. It is the one who has true friends, ones who have our back when we are down. Ones who don't mind sharing their last bite of chocolate. Ones who will take our secrets to the grave. I was praying once, and God whispered to me that friends were like gold—it isn't the quantity of the gold that is important; it is the quality.

Epilogue
The Blessing

Wisdom hath builded her house, she hath hewn out her seven pillars.

Proverbs 9:1

Happy is the man that findeth wisdom, and the man that getteth understanding.

Proverbs 3:13

Receive my instruction, and not silver; and knowledge rather than choice gold. For wisdom is better than rubies; and all the things that may be desired are not to be compared to it.

Proverbs 8:10-11

But speak thou the things which become sound doctrine: That the aged men be sober, grave, temperate, sound in faith, in charity, in patience. The aged women likewise, that they be in behaviour as becometh holiness, not false accusers, not given to much wine, teachers of good things; that they may teach the young women to be sober, to love their husbands, to love their children, to be discreet, chaste, keepers at home, good, obedient to their own husbands, that the word of God be not blasphemed. Young men likewise exhort to be sober minded. In all things shewing thyself a pattern of good works: in doctrine shewing uncorruptness, gravity, sincerity.

Titus 2:1-7

Finally, Beloved, permit me, an "older" woman, to relay to you some parting words of wisdom. These seven pillars of a house built with wisdom are tried and true. They will stand the test of time in our homes if we will give them a chance. Our children are our greatest gift and our greatest responsibility—they are more precious than gold.

When taught correctly and given the proper tools, they are a joy. They are the gift that keeps on giving in the currency of grandchildren. Just when we think our children are the best thing since sliced bread, along comes the grandchildren, and, well...think warm homemade, drenched with warm real butter, so good you want to slap your mamma bread—that's grandchildren! It can't get any better than that!

This book is meant to be a tool for parents. Our final authority in parenting should always be the Word of God. His Word is alive and sharper than any two-edged sword. Our deepest desire is to see happy homes all over this world. Our hope and prayer is that everyone will take the tools in this book and start building strong, healthy, loving, and lasting relationships with their children. Our children are worth our time.

If our child gets arrested or gets into trouble, wouldn't we hire the best lawyer we could afford? We would sell anything we had to sell and do anything we had to do to get our child out of trouble.

Beloved, it never has to come to that. We need to do what is needed now. We don't need a fancy lawyer to rescue our children; we need God's Word. When parenting is at its best, our children will not be in need of a legal defense team—just a good parenting team.

It is more cost-effective to do upkeep on a home than it is to call a repairman after something breaks. Let's not wait to get our priorities in order. God is tremendously patient, but, Beloved, we have wasted enough years doing it the wrong way. Time is short, and we want to be diligent and work while there is still some sunshine left in the day.

We have heard it said more than once that a man (or woman), when faced with death, never says he wished he would have spent more time at work. He always grieves not having spent quality time with his family.

We must be consistent in all that we say and do. We don't want to be like the reed shaken in the wind, tossed to and fro. Nor do we want to be like the house of straw or sticks, ready to crumble at a puff of air.

Instead, let us be a house made of bricks—a house that will stand the storms of life. We want a house that is thoughtfully built, brick upon brick, with the same consistency day after day. Such a house will weather any hurricane life may toss its way. When all the other houses fall, this one will stand strong.

We must always demonstrate right behavior for our children. We are their first teacher. Let's go for teacher of the year every year.

Be a trustworthy parent. We must be true to our word every time. An obedient child is one who knows we are trustworthy. There is a sense of pride in children when they can say, "My dad said he would, and he always keeps his promises."

Our children's lives depend on the words we speak to them and about them. Speak honestly and kindly. Never say something about your child that you don't want to come to pass. The words we speak about our children today will be the same words they will speak about their children tomorrow. The next generation cries out to us, "Choose those words carefully; our lives depend on them."

Let us revisit etiquette and good manners, going back to the foundations of our American culture, when manners were required and self-control didn't need to be taught at school; it was demonstrated and expected at home. The time when a young man opened the door for a lady, and the lady graciously accepted. When young children didn't interrupt and overtake an adult conversation. When cursing was used only in poolrooms and bars, not in stores or churches. When we ate to live and did not live to eat. When young people showed respect for their elders, and the elders passed on pearls of great wisdom.

Let us go back to the time when a tantrum was not a socially accepted behavior, and when the parents ran the home, not the children. Let us go back to our righteous roots to a time when conversations were not coarse and suggestive. We must take back our homes. Self-control has been misplaced, but not lost. It has been missing for a few years, but it has not vanished. For the sake of our children and for the sake of the future generations, we must again demonstrate and teach self-control.

Show me your friends; I'll show you your future. The pillar of association is not an option in building a sturdy home for our children—it is a parental responsibility, a responsibility to be taken with seriousness and great consideration. Our children's friends hold a place of great significance; they are more important than what our child wears or eats. Parenting is about choices and wisdom; they go hand in hand. We are not going to always make the right choice or always use the greatest wisdom, but if we try our best and repent when we miss it, we will succeed.

We must give our children the same benefit that we want others to give us. They, too, can have a rough day. Remember dodge ball? School can be rough. We might miss too many questions on a test, or forget to do our homework, or lose our pencil. It is tough sometimes. We're not raising clones; we are teaching our children how to succeed in life. They will disappoint us. We will disappoint them. We have all disappointed people whom we love and have been disappointed ourselves by those same people, but we don't stop loving, and we don't stop trying to get it right.

Beloved, don't cry over the $4 gallon of spilled milk. Let's let it go—it is not important. Let's smile when our children least expect it, and never raise our voices to try to teach them something. Enjoy them. The next time we blink, they will be grown.

Great rewards call for a great investment. Our children's lives are the best investment we will ever make. They don't want a room full of stuff; they just want our love. They don't need expensive vacations; they just need our time.

God gave these children to us because He believed He could trust us with them. He knew we had what it takes to parent them the way they need to be parented. He believed we would nourish their gifts and callings. He knew we were the right people for the biggest job He had—raising His children.

If God believes in us and our abilities so strongly, who are we to say the Creator of the universe is wrong? Now, we need to believe in our children and their future the way God believes in us.

Beloved, I wish above all that you and your family would prosper. It has been my greatest privilege to share with you what God has allowed me to learn in my family over the years.

I pray that as you build your home on these seven pillars, you will obtain great wisdom, and in that wisdom, you will find understanding for your life and your children's lives. I pray that you are balanced in all things that you say and do. May your homes and your lives be filled with great peace and pleasant rest.

Be blessed!

About the Author

LINDA HORTON IS THE founder of Dynamic Family Life Ministries. Linda's passion is for people to realize true peace and happiness in every aspect of their lives. Her focus is on parents: equipping them to be the best they can be and providing the tools they need to raise successful children and productive citizens.

Linda is an ordained minister. She received her Bachelor's Degree in Christian Education from Shalom Bible College and Seminary and is currently finishing her Master's Degree in Counseling.

At the age of fifteen, Linda found her calling teaching children; she has never stopped. She is an enthusiastic guardian of the parent's right to home school. She has worked diligently to educate and facilitate families in all aspects of education, keeping the needs of the children first and foremost.

Linda has pioneered two Christian schools as well as taught and advised private schools on curriculum, testing, discipline, and policy.

Linda is happily married to her husband of thirty years, Dennis, who is her strongest supporter and dearest friend. They reside in Port Saint Lucie, Florida. She is the proud mother of four sons, Mathew,

Mark, Michael, and Timothy, and two daughters-in-love, Amber and Tiffany. She is the most blessed and grateful to be the Mamaw of four grandchildren, Micah, Lydia, Grace, and the fourth—yet to be born, but sure to be a blessing.

You may contact Linda via email at **DFLM@bellsouth.net** or visit the ministry web site at: www.dynamicfamilylife.org.

If you're a fan of this book, please tell others...

- Write about *The Seven Pillars of Parenting* on your blog, Twitter, MySpace, or Facebook page.
- Suggest *The Seven Pillars of Parenting* to friends.
- When you're in a bookstore, ask them if they carry the book and if not, suggest that they order it.
- Write a review of *The Seven Pillars of Parenting* on www.amazon.com.
- Email suggestions to **DFLM@bellsouth.net** on websites, conferences, and events you know of where this book could be offered.
- Purchase additional copies to give away as gifts.

Connect with me...

If you'd like to learn more about *The Seven Pillars of Parenting* or my ministry, Dynamic Family Life Ministries, check out my website at www.dynamicfamilylife.org. You can also contact my Publisher directly:

HigherLife Development Services
2342 Westminster Terrace
Oviedo, Florida 32765
Phone: (407) 563-4806
Email: info@ahigherlife.com